INSIGHT COMPACT GUIDE

BRUGES

Compact Guide: Bruges is the ultimate quick-reference guide to this Belgian jewel. It tells you everything you need to know about the city's attractions, from the details of its facades to the grandeur of its squares, from the tranquillity of its canals and almshouses to the treasures of its churches and museums.

This is one of 133 Compact Guides produced by the editors of Insight Guides, whose books have set the standard for visual travel guides since 1970. Packed with information, arranged in easy-to-follow routes, and lavishly illustrated with photographs, this book not only steers you round Bruges but also gives you fascinating insights into local life.

Insight Compact Guide: Bruges

Written by: George McDonald
Photography by: Jerry Dennis
Additional photography by: Tony Halliday; 13/1 Eric Lessing/ AKG-images London
Cover picture by: Robert Harding Picture Library
Picture Editor: Hilary Genin
Maps: Graham Sendall and Maria Donnelly

Editorial Director: Brian Bell
Managing Editor: Tony Halliday

CONTACTING THE EDITORS: As every effort is made to provide accurate information in this publication, we would appreciate it if readers would call our attention to any errors and omissions by contacting:
Apa Publications, PO Box 7910, London SE1 1WE, England.
Fax: (44 20) 7403 0290
e-mail: insight@apaguide.co.uk

Information has been obtained from sources believed to be reliable, but its accuracy and completeness, and the opinions based thereon, are not guaranteed.

Second Edition 2001; Updated 2006
Printed in Singapore by Insight Print Services (Pte) Ltd

Worldwide distribution enquiries:
APA Publications GmbH & Co. Verlag KG (Singapore Branch)
38 Joo Koon Road, Singapore 628990
Tel: (65) 6865-1600, Fax: (65) 6861-6438

Distributed in the UK & Ireland by:
GeoCenter International Ltd
The Viables Centre, Harrow Way, Basingstoke,
Hampshire RG22 4BJ
Tel: (44 1256) 817987, Fax: (44 1256) 817-988

Distributed in the United States by:
Langenscheidt Publishers, Inc.
36-36 33rd Street 4th Floor,
Long Island City, New York 11106
Tel: (1 718) 784-0055, Fax: (1 718) 784-0640

www.insightguides.com
In North America:
www.insighttravelguides.com

BRUGES

Introduction

Places

Culture

Travel Tips

▷ **Rozenhoedkaai view (p33)** Countless artists have painted this scene, across the canal with the towering Belfry in the background.

△ **Halve Maan (p45)** A notable brewery, whose beer can be sampled on the premises.

▷ **Lace Centre (p60)** Find out more about this traditional Flanders craft.

▽ **Royal Tombs (p38)** The tombs of Mary of Burgundy and Charles the Bold are symbolic of the city's medieval prowess.

▷ **St John's Hospital (p44)** This huge medieval complex today houses the famous Memling Museum.

▷ **Groeninge Museum (p34)** With its collection of 'Flemish Primitives', this art museum is a real jewel.

△ **Burg (p22–26)** One of Bruges' two main squares, whose highlights include the Town Hall's Gothic Hall (here a mural).

▽ **Jerusalem Church (p59)** Inspired by the Church of the Holy Sepulchre, this was built by a wealthy local family.

▷ **Markt (p27–30)** The other square features the Belfry and this statue of two local heroes, and is a popular meeting place.

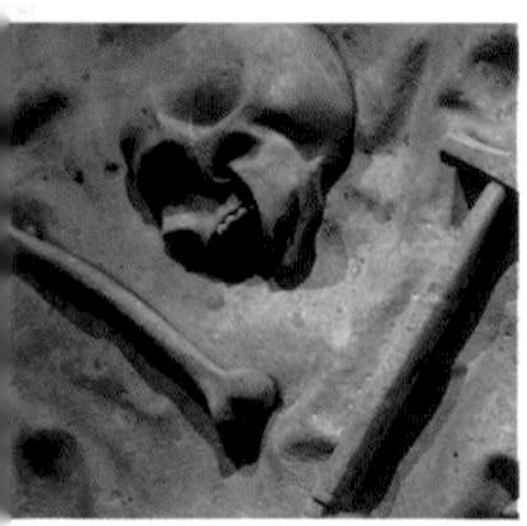

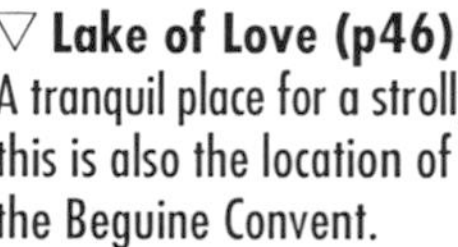

▽ **Lake of Love (p46)** A tranquil place for a stroll, this is also the location of the Beguine Convent.

Brugge – Travels In Time

There is nowhere quite like Bruges. Those gabled houses, meandering canals and narrow cobblestone streets together produce one of the most romantic towns in Europe. Those who speak of it as the 'Venice of the North' or 'Belgium's Amsterdam', or make some other fanciful comparison, do no service to the city, nor do they add anything useful to visitors' understanding or appreciation of the place. Bruges, situated in the heart of the northern part of Belgium called Flanders, is simply unique and simply itself. It is not some pale imitation of another place and needs no such false comparisons to illuminate it.

Opposite: transport at the Markt
Below: Wollestraat window
Bottom: canal cruise

Flemish Identity

What is it then? Well, for a start it isn't really Bruges at all: it's 'Brugge'. On a practical level, if you want to get off at the right railway station, you have to think 'Brugge' and not Bruges, since that's what's written on the station destination boards. If you want to get even a little way below the surface of life here you absolutely must try to think 'Brugge' and not Bruges. The city is the pride and joy of Flanders, and just below the smoothly cosmopolitan surface with which it greets its legions of foreign admirers, it is Flemish through and through (in this book, however, we will accept linguistic reality and use the familiar anglicised – or frenchified – name).

Like most visitors, you'll probably end up describing this canal-threaded ensemble of medieval architecture as 'picturesque'. There's an almost unreal quality to just how stagily pretty Bruges can be, as if in the Middle Ages the city had been a place of universal grace and effortless charm instead of the noisy, smelly sink it probably was.

Should Bruges have a weak point, this is it. A city that looks and feels like a museum can be hard to get close to, however grateful we might be that it has come safely down through the centuries to us. After a while you might even get to miss

Sightseeing made easy Almost everything that visitors want to see and do lies within the ring canal, and in fact occupies a core zone within that. Distances are not great, which makes getting to see a lot relatively easy, even if you're on a tight schedule.

the kind of gritty urban reality that gives other Flemish cities like Ghent and Antwerp a more fully developed character. If this is a criticism then it is not exactly an onerous one. Certainly no one from Bruges will blame you for setting aside competing philosophies of urban existence and simply getting on with the business of enjoying your stay in their city.

OPEN-AIR MUSEUM

Prize exhibit

Only after visiting Bruges, the grand old lady of Flemish cities, can you begin to understand Flanders and begin to grasp the many-faceted heritage which the French and Burgundians, Germans and English, Spanish and Austrians have left in this enigmatic part of northwest Europe. Flanders would be a very different place without Bruges to remind it of its glorious past. We shouldn't get too starry-eyed, though, over this image of a city frozen in time. Bruges is slickly professional in packaging tourism in a medieval glaze, and its tourist industry is equally adept at separating – for the most part painlessly – visitors from their cash.

That said, one of the most remarkable facets of life in Bruges is the almost unfailing politeness of the population. The natives really are friendly. Considering that they have to go about their everyday lives in this open-air museum, tripping over hordes of tourists every day of the year, this could hardly be taken for granted.

POSITION AND LAYOUT

Bruges has a population of 120,000, of whom 50,000 live in the old city, and lies on the edge of the Flemish polder (land reclaimed from the sea) 88km (55 miles) northwest of Brussels, 92km (57 miles) west of Antwerp, and 46km (28 miles) northwest of Ghent. It lies just 14km (9 miles) south of the busy ferry port and commercial harbour of Zeebrugge, which is itself close to the northern end of Belgium's 64km-long (40-mile) North Sea coast.

The city has two connected hearts in the side-by-side monumental squares called the Markt and the Burg. Narrow streets fan out from these two squares, and a network of canals threads its way to nearly every section of the small city. The centre is almost encircled by a canal and a ring road that follow the line of the now demolished city walls. The canal opens at its southern end to become the Minnewater (Lake of Love), filled with swans and other birds, and bordered by the Begijnhof and the Minnewater Park. On the outer side of the Minnewater is the railway station.

CLIMATE CHART

Bruges

°C J F M A M J J A S O N D mm

25 20 15 10 5 0 -5

100 80 60 40 20 0

Maximum temperature
Minimum temperature
Rainfall
Sunny months
Rainy months

CLIMATE AND WHEN TO GO

The best time to visit is from April to October: the weather is (generally) better and museums and other attractions are open longer then. But Bruges can get very crowded during this period, particularly during July and August. Spring and autumn are also good times to visit. The city is far less busy in winter; if you are lucky, it might be cold enough for you to be able to skate on the canals.

THE CANALS

It's a good idea to take a canal-boat trip, as the canals, known as *reien,* provide the best vantage point for viewing the city. You cover many of

View from Rozenhoedkaai, the Belfry in the background

the same places as on a walking tour, but from a uniquely satisfying angle. On a warm and sunny day there is no better or easier way of seeing the city than from an open-topped boat.

A good thing about the boat tour is that it gives you a brief overview of the historic centre, allowing you to zero in later on a section you fancied, without having to walk your socks off in the search. Yet walk you should, as far and as often as possible, to see Bruges at a human pace and to feel the legacy of 1,000 years.

Those canals connect with the vast European inland waterway system. If you are visiting by boat, you can move on to almost anywhere on the Continent from here.

Below: eating out on Guido-Gezelleplein
Bottom: Leda and Zeus sculpture on Walplein

WALKING LEGEND

Bruges is a small city which actively discourages cars in the centre, so it is pleasant to walk through its old central district. But it is also interesting to get a feel for Bruges outside the centre (though staying within the ring canal), a zone that has its fair share of historical treasures. The lucky inhabitants just live in it, not particularly dressing it up for the benefit of the tourists, though it is picture-book pretty almost everywhere. Bruges rewards aimless wanderers as well as itinerary-followers, so it's a good idea to try to

spend some time just strolling around the streets, keeping your eyes open and your guidebook closed, making your own discoveries.

In fact, there is more to the city than its historic legacy. While walking (or cycling if you prefer, *see page 114*) the routes in this book, take time out to observe the things that don't make for thrilling exposition but do add a human dimension of everyday life, without which the city will seem like something preserved in aspic. There are other shops, for example, than those selling lace, diamonds, antiques and handmade pralines, even if it often seems as though there aren't. You'll find quaint chemists, fashion-conscious boutiques, hardware stores, music stores, video clubs. There are even some discreet sex clubs, although there is not a well-defined red-light district.

Early prosperity

The city's early prosperity depended on its role as the chief port of Flanders, a hub of the English and Scandinavian trade. From the Roman period to the 11th century, ships sailed right into the centre on the River Reie; later, sea-going ships went as far as Damme, while smaller vessels handled canal traffic between Bruges and Damme. It was also one of the most important textile centres in northwest Europe. So wealthy was Bruges that when the French Queen Joan of Navarre visited in 1301, she complained that hundreds of women were as finely dressed as she.

ECONOMY AND INDUSTRY

Historically, Bruges was a trading city, the economic capital of northwest Europe from 1200 to 1400 and still a major player well into the 1500s. When the Zwin inlet in the Western Scheldt estuary silted up in the 1520s, blocking off Bruges' outlet to the sea, the encroaching sands also choked a prosperity that had seemed destined to last for ever.

It was politics that dealt the knockout blow, however. After Bruges rebelled against the Habsburg Empire in the shape of Crown Prince Maximilian in 1482, locking him up and removing the head of his top adviser, the empire struck back by replacing Bruges with Ghent as the local royal residence, and transferring the city's trading privileges to Antwerp. The Spanish Habsburgs' subsequent savage campaigns to suppress Protestantism and rebellion in the Low Countries during the late 16th and early 17th centuries set the seal on economic decline.

The Industrial Revolution mostly passed Bruges by, leaving it a quaint and impoverished backwater by the time Belgium won its independence from Holland in 1830. It wasn't until the harbour at Zeebrugge was completed in 1904

Below: distinguished shop signs

Character preserved
Today, we can see that the city's long economic decline and fall was a blessing in disguise, a beneficial outcome of the law of unintended consequences. During all those centuries Bruges could not afford to alter or reconstruct its Gothic character. As a result, we have it all – or at any rate much of it – still to see and enjoy. Bruges also owes much to the fact that it was spared the bombs of World War II. It was on the German target list, but on the intended night, while approaching Bruges, the squadron leader radioed the order that no bombs were to be dropped on the historic centre. He returned for a visit in the year 2000 and was duly honoured by the grateful citizens of Bruges.

Knight at the entrance to the Basilica of the Holy Blood

and connected to Bruges by canal, thus re-establishing the all-important link with the sea after almost four centuries, that the local economy started showing genuine signs of life again – proof of how its prosperity was linked with trade.

Since the end of World War II, tourism has become the main engine of prosperity. The city's architectural heritage was actually in poor and declining shape until well into the 1960s. Vast Gothic buildings need vast amounts of looking after and a lot of money to pay for doing it, and small Gothic buildings also add up to a refurbishing headache when there are so many of them. The process of stabilising the 'look' of Bruges is still going on and, although much of the heavy lifting has now been done, there are places in outlying parts of town that still look decrepit.

HISTORICAL PERIODS

Bruges is almost all about history, and history (especially other people's) can be an indigestible dish. Just look at the glazed expressions on the faces of tourists trying to take in a thumbnail-sketch account on their guided tours: it's not entirely surprising if they get their Charles the Bolds mixed up with their Benedictine nuns and Burgundian celebrations. While all historical divisions are to some extent arbitrary – in that for ordinary people life usually went on much as before, whichever bunch of self-inflated bluebloods occupied the Castle of the Counts or the Prinsenhof – they at least help provide a sense of perspective across the centuries.

First on the scene as the mists of the Dark Ages began to disperse were the Counts of Flanders, who established the city of Bruges and went on to rule it as if it were their own personal fiefdom – as in fact it was. They lasted from some time in the 8th century until 1384. Highlights of their glorious career include the murder of Count Charles the Good, the supposed return of a Relic of the Holy Blood from the Holy Land by Count Thierry of Alsace, and the death of the last of them, Count Louis of Male, in 1384.

Next up were the Dukes of Burgundy, an ambitious family, whose seat had been in Dijon until one of them, Philip the Bold, married Louis of Male's daughter and heir, thereby pocketing Flanders when Louis died, and eventually adding most of the Low Countries to what was an empire. The Burgundians lasted until 1482, when the fatal fall from a horse of Charles the Bold's daughter and heir, Mary, pitched Flanders, and Bruges, into the hands of her husband, Crown Prince Maximilian of the Austrian House of Habsburg.

Below: Charles the Bold
Bottom: carving on the Episcopal Palace

ENTER SPAIN...EXIT FRANCE

Their son Philip the Handsome married Joan the Mad of Spain, thereby retaining the penchant for bizarre monikers and bringing Spain into the Habsburg fold. The high point for Flanders was in 1516, when at the age of 15 Charles V, born in Ghent, inherited the empire. After him came heavy-handed Spanish then Austrian Habsburgs, until the Revolutionary French ended this part of the tale by occupying Bruges in 1794.

The by then Napoleonic French were ejected in turn in 1814, and Bruges became part of the Kingdom of the Netherlands. Although far from popular, the Dutch managed to hold on until 1830, when Belgium's short, if not sweet, War of Independence was fought and won.

HISTORICAL HIGHLIGHTS

1st century BC Celtic farmers are established on the coastal plain around what is now Bruges.

1st century AD A Gallo-Roman settlement is founded beside the Rivers Reie and Dijver, and maintains trading links with Britain and Gaul.

8th century St Eloy writes of the *municipium Flandrense*, an important town in the Flemish coastal plain, which seems likely to have been Bruges.

circa 850 A fort is built in the town for defence against attacks by Viking raiders.

861 Baldwin Iron Arm, the first Count of Flanders whose name is known, elopes with the daughter of Carolingian King Charles the Bald.

864 The first record of the name 'Bruggia – a melding of the Old Norse *bryggja* (jetty) and Rugja, the original name of the River Reie – appears on coins of Charles the Bald.

c940 Count Arnulf I develops the Burg, building his castle and the Church of St Donatian there.

c1040 An English text calls Bruges an important maritime trading centre, but by the end of the century access to the sea is closed by silting.

1127 Count Charles the Good is murdered in St Donatian's. Bruges is granted its first charter, and building of the city wall begins.

1134 Flooding creates a channel, the Zwin, from the sea to Damme. Bruges builds a canal to Damme, reopening a maritime trading route.

1150 Count Thierry of Alsace is said to bring back from the Second Crusade a relic of the Blood of Christ.

1177 Bruges is granted a revised charter by Count Philip of Alsace.

1200s Some of Bruges' most prominent buildings, including the Belfry, Market Halls, Begijnhof and St John's Hospital, are begun.

1250 With a population of 40–50,000, Bruges is among the biggest and richest cities in northwest Europe, through trade and textiles manufacture.

1297 King Philip IV of France annexes Flanders. New fortifications are begun.

1302 Weaver Pieter de Coninck and butcher Jan Breidel foment rebellion against France. French citizens and sympathisers are massacred in the 'Bruges Matins', and an army of Flemish peasants and craftsmen slaughters the French knights at the Battle of the Golden Spurs.

1305 The war with France ends in a treaty that is unfavourable to Flanders. Bruges' defences are dismantled.

1316 Famine strikes the city, killing thousands; 33 years later thousands more lives are lost in a plague.

1376 Building of the Town Hall begins, at a time of great prosperity from international trade.

1384 Count Louis is succeeded by his daughter Margaret, wife of Philip the Bold, Duke of Burgundy. The dazzling Burgundian century begins.

1400s Cloth-making declines, but prosperity continues from trade and banking.

1430 Duke Philip the Good founds the Order of the Golden Fleece in Bruges.

1436 Jan van Eyck paints the *Virgin and Child.*

1436–8 Philip the Good cruelly crushes a rebellion against him in Bruges.

1474–9 Hans Memling paints the *Triptych of St John.*

1477 Death of Duke Charles the Bold sparks another rebellion. His successor, Mary of Burgundy, wife of Habsburg Crown Prince Maximilian of Austria, grants the city a new charter.

1482 After Mary's death in a riding accident, Bruges rebels against its new Habsburg rulers. The ducal residence is moved to Ghent.

1520 The Zwin silts up Bruges' access to the sea triggering economic decline.

1527 Bruges' first Protestant martyr is burned at the stake in the Burg.

1559 The Bishopric of Bruges is established.

1577 Bruges hesitantly joins the Low Countries' rebellion against Spanish rule.

1580 The city signs the Treaty of Utrecht against Spain; Protestantism becomes the only permitted religion.

1584 Spain re-establishes control. Many Protestants flee to Holland. The following year the Scheldt estuary is blockaded and Bruges goes into steep decline.

1622 Opening of a canal to Ostend gives Bruges an outlet to the sea again.

1744–8 Bruges is occupied by the French.

1753 The Coupure Canal opened, allowing sea-going vessels into the city centre.

1794–5 Revolutionary France occupies the city. Many churches and monasteries destroyed.

1815 Napoleon defeated at Waterloo. Bruges becomes part of the Kingdom of the Netherlands.

1830 Bruges joins the Southern Netherlands' revolt against Dutch rule, becoming part of the Kingdom of Belgium.

1847 Hunger riots erupt in Bruges, the poorest city in Belgium.

1892 Georges Rodenbach's novel *Bruges-la-Morte* is published.

1892 The Flemish poet Guido Gezelle dies in the city.

1904 A new harbour at Zeebrugge is completed.

1914–18 World War I. Germans occupy Bruges for four years, destroying Zeebrugge harbour as they retreat.

1940–44 World War II. Germans occupy Bruges for 4½ years, again destroying Zeebrugge harbour as they retreat.

1950s Modern tourist boom begins.

1971 Bruges merges with surrounding municipalities, making it Flanders' third biggest city.

1997 The city centre is made virtually car-free.

2002 Bruges is a cultural capital of Europe for a year; the Concertgebouw concert hall opens.

2004 Triennial Reie Festival takes place.

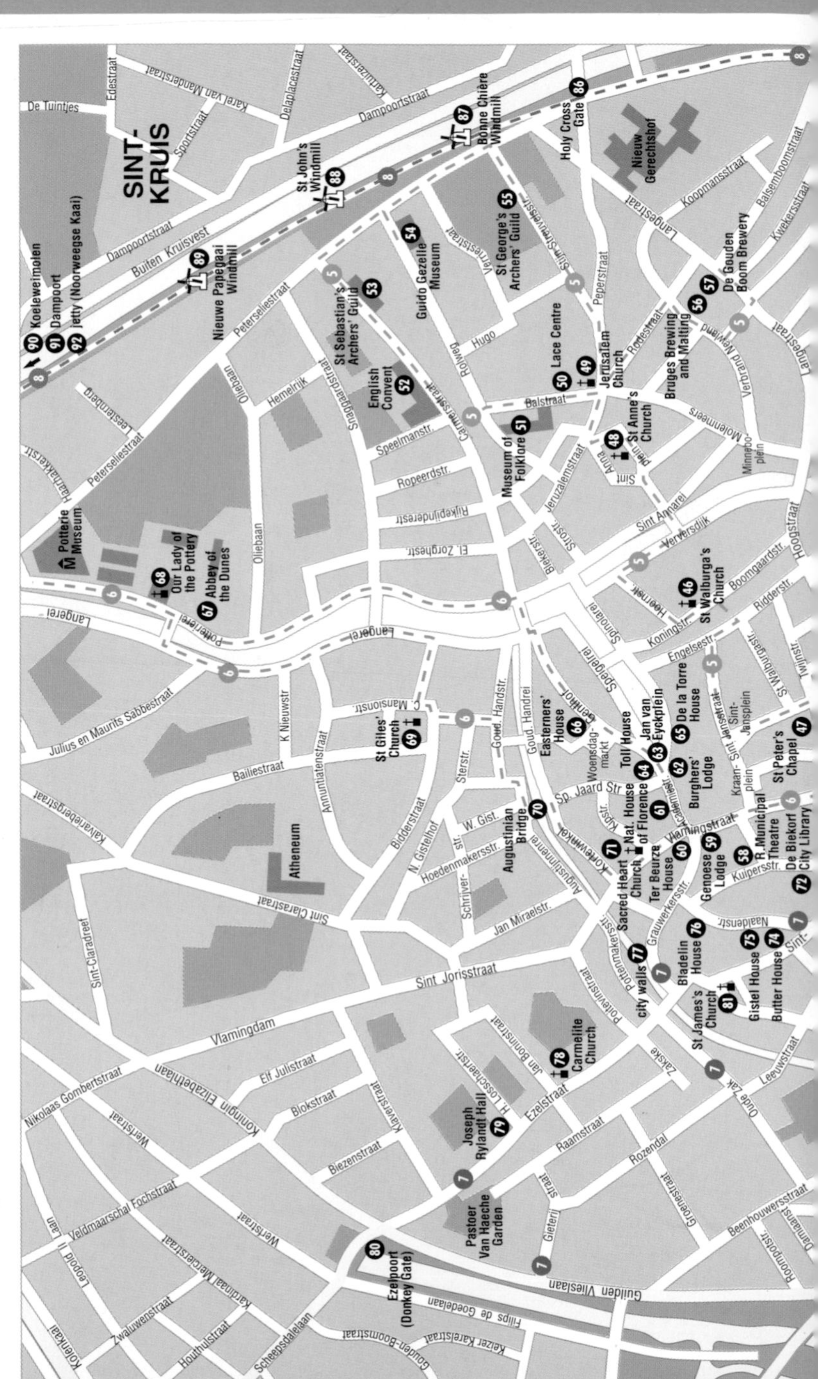

SINT-KRUIS
90 Koeleweimolen
91 Dampoort
92 Jetty (Noorweegse Kaai)
89 Nieuwe Papegaai Windmill
88 St John's Windmill
87 Bonne Chière Windmill
86 Holy Cross Gate
Nieuw Gerechtshof
55 St George's Archers' Guild
54 Guido Gezelle Museum
53 St Sebastian's Archers' Guild
52 English Convent
50 Lace Centre
49 Jerusalem Church
51 Museum of Folklore
48 St Anne's Church
56 57 De Gouden Boom Brewery
Bruges Brewing and Malting
Potterie Museum
68 Our Lady of the Pottery
67 Abbey of the Dunes
46 St Walburga's Church
69 St Giles' Church
66 Easterners' House
64 Toll House
63 Jan van Eyckplein
65 De la Torre House
62 Burghers' Lodge
61 Nat. House of Florence
70 Augustinian Bridge
71 Sacred Heart Church
60 Ter Beurze House
59 Genoese Lodge
58 R. Municipal Theatre
72 De Biekorf City Library
47 St Peter's Chapel
Atheneum
77 city walls
76 Bladelin House
75 Gistel House
74 Butter House
81 St James's Church
78 Carmelite Church
79 Joseph Ryelandt Hall
Pastoer Van Haeche Garden
80 Ezelpoort (Donkey Gate)
Dampoortstraat
Buiten Kruisvest
Peterseliestraat
Langerei
Potterierei
Julius en Maurits Sabbestraat
Baliestraat
Sint Clarastraat
Sint Jorisstraat
Vlamingdam
Koningin Elizabethlaan
Nikolaas Gombertstraat
Ezelstraat
Langestraat
Spiegelrei
Gulden Vlieslaan
Vlamingstraat
Kortewinkel
Carmersstraat
Balstraat
Peperstraat
Sint Annarei
Verversdijk

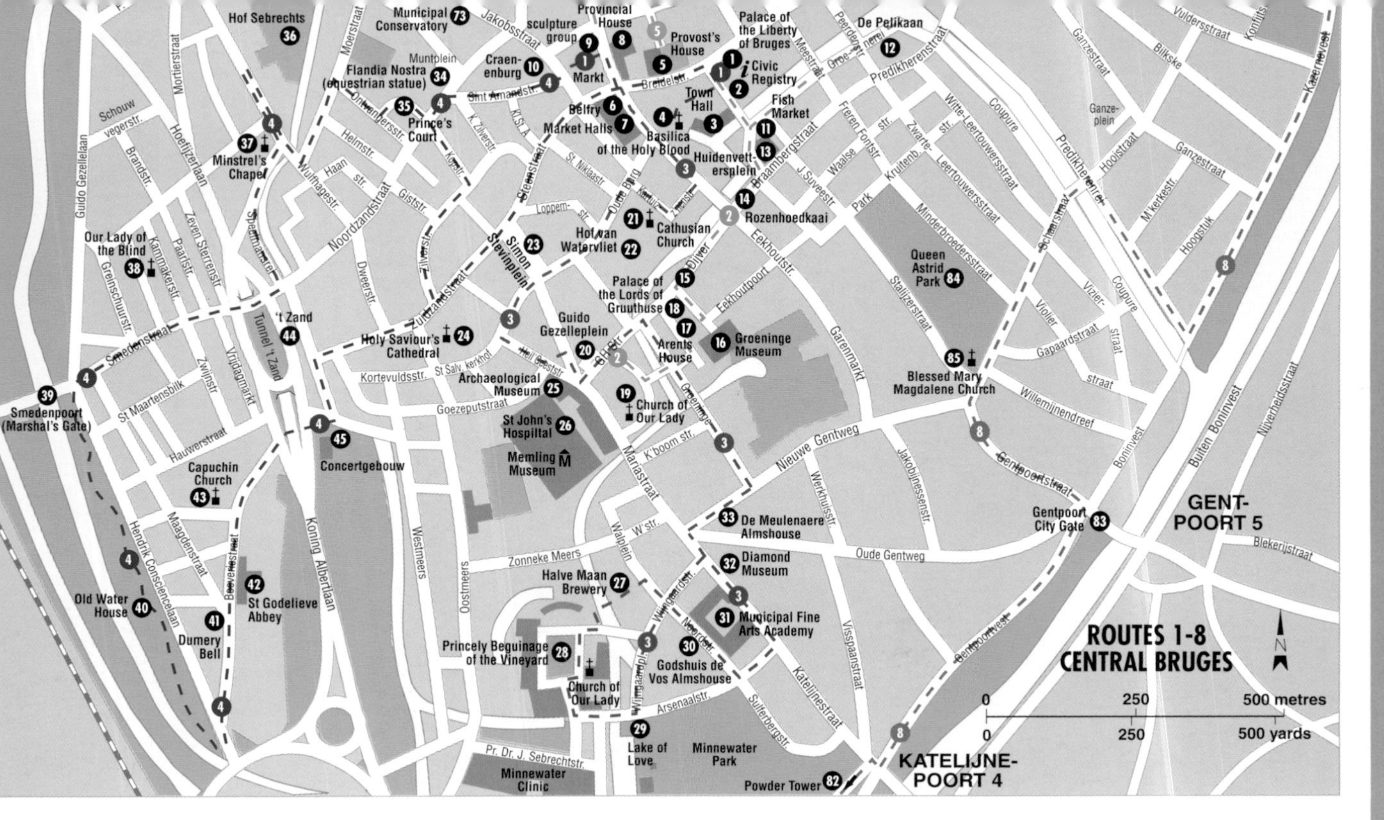
ROUTES 1-8
CENTRAL BRUGES
0
250
500 metres
0
250
500 yards
N
GENT-
POORT 5
KATELIJNE-
POORT 4
Gentpoort City Gate
Blessed Mary Magdalene Church
Queen Astrid Park
De Pelikaan
Palace of the Liberty of Bruges
Civic Registry
Fish Market
Provost's House
Town Hall
Basilica of the Holy Blood
Huidenvettersplein
Rozenhoedkaai
Provincial House
Markt
Belfry
Market Halls
Cathusian Church
Hof van Watervliet
Palace of the Lords of Gruuthuse
Groeninge Museum
Arents House
Church of Our Lady
Guido Gezelleplein
sculpture group
Craenenburg
Simon Stevinplein
Holy Saviour's Cathedral
Archaeological Museum
St John's Hospital
Memling Museum
De Meulenaere Almshouse
Diamond Museum
Municipal Fine Arts Academy
Godshuis de Vos Almshouse
Halve Maan Brewery
Princely Beguinage of the Vineyard
Church of Our Lady
Lake of Love
Minnewater Park
Powder Tower
Minnewater Clinic
Municipal Conservatory
Flandia Nostra (equestrian statue)
Prince's Court
Hof Sebrechts
Minstrel's Chapel
't Zand
Tunnel 't Zand
Concertgebouw
St Godelieve Abbey
Capuchin Church
Dumery Bell
Old Water House
Our Lady of the Blind
Smedenpoort (Marshal's Gate)
Kazernevest
Nijverheidsstraat
Buiten Boninvest
Blekerijstraat
Boninvest
Gentpoortvest
Gentpoortstraat
Coupure
Predikherenrei
Ganzestraat
Ganzeplein
Hoogstuk
M'kerkestr.
Hooistraat
Vuldersstraat
Bilkske
Violier
Vizier-straat
Gapaardstraat
Willemijnendreef
Minderbroedersstraat
Leertouwersstraat
Witte-Leertouwersstraat
Stalijzerstraat
Jakobijnessenstr.
Oude Gentweg
Nieuwe Gentweg
Garenmarkt
Park
Visspaanstraat
Werkhuisstr.
Katelijnestraat
Sulferbergstr.
Arsenaalstr.
Wijngaardplein
Wijngaardstr.
Walplein
Mariastraat
Zonneke Meers
Oostmeers
Westmeers
Pr. Dr. J. Sebrechtsstr.
Peerdenstr.
Predikherenstraat
Meestraat
Freren Fontstr.
Waalse
J. Suveestr.
Braambergstraat
Eekhoutstr.
Eekhoutpoort
Dijver
Groeninge
Oude Burg
Steenstraat
Jakobsstraat
Kl. St. A.
K. Zilverstr.
Zilverstr.
Zuidzandstraat
Heilig Geeststr.
St Salv. kerkhof
Kortevuldersstr.
Goezeputstraat
Dweerstr.
Noordzandstraat
Moerstraat
Wulfhagestr.
Helmstr.
Gistst.
Muntplein
Koning Albertlaan
Speelmansrei
Vrijdagmarkt
Zwijnstr
Zeven Sterrenstr
Hoefijzerlaan
Paarlstr.
Kammakerstr.
Brandstr.
Vegerstr.
Schouw
Greinschuurstr.
Guido Gezellelaan
Smedenstraat
St Maartensbilk
Hauwerstraat
Maagdenstraat
Boeverievestraat
Hendrik Consciencelaan
Mortierstraat

1: The Heart of Bruges

Palace of the Liberty of Bruges – Hall of the Liberty of Bruges – Town Hall – Basilica of the Holy Blood – Provost's House – Belfry – Market Halls – Provincial House – Sculpture of Jan Breydel and Pieter de Coninck – Craenenburg

Preceding pages: reflections along the Potterierei
Below: inside the Gothic Hall
Bottom: gathering on the Burg

Bruges actually has two hearts. Both are ancient monumental squares: one is called the Burg and the other the Markt, and they are connected by Breidelstraat. In each one of them the pulse of the Middle Ages beats strongly, and despite the inevitable changes that the centuries have wrought, they are among the best places to experience Bruges' direct connection to its glorious past, when emperors held court here.

THE BURG

The ★★★**Burg** is Bruges' most historic square and the ideal place to begin your discovery of the city. This is where, in the mid-9th century, Baldwin Iron Arm, Count of Flanders, built a castle or 'burg', the Steen (since demolished), around which a village developed. It has always been the civic and religious heart of the city. Side by side in this relatively small cobbled square stands a harmonious array of marvellous buildings that span the centuries, from the 12th to the 19th, in a fascinating trip down

architecture's memory lane. There are even some reasonable efforts from the 20th century (the Crowne Plaza Brugge Hotel, *see page 26*) for example. Popular events, including burnings at the stake and beheadings, were often held in the Burg.

Star Attractions
- **Burg**
- **Palace of the Liberty of Bruges**

PALACE OF THE LIBERTY OF BRUGES

The ★★ **Palace of the Liberty of Bruges** (Landhuis van het Brugse Vrije) ❶ closes off one side of the Square. Down through the centuries, the citizens of Bruges have taken great care of their civic liberties, cherishing them to the point of rebellion against any authority that presumed to scorn them.

In this case, however, the Liberty after which this palace was named was a geographical concept. It referred to the district around the city, which from the early Middle Ages was a castellany of the County of Flanders, stretching to the coast and rich enough – with Bruges, Ghent and Ieper (Ypres) – to be separately represented after 1127 at the Flemish Estates (a kind of early parliament).

In the right light
Photographers who want to catch the Town Hall in the Burg and the Belfry in the Markt at their best, should wait until late afternoon when the sun shines on them at the front – assuming there is any sun, that is.

NEOCLASSICAL STYLE

When, in the late 14th century, the Dukes of Burgundy vacated their damp and draughty 11th-century wooden residence on the Burg and decamped across town to the Prinsenhof *(see page 50)*, the Liberty promptly moved its administration into the empty space. Further construction in the 15th century extended it southwards towards the Groenerei canal. From 1520 to 1525 the crumbling old residence was rebuilt as the Palace of the Liberty. Most of it was further rebuilt in neoclassical style from 1722 to 1727 by the Amsterdam architect Jan Verkruys.

Following Bruges' occupation by Revolutionary France in 1794, the Liberty, along with much of the old regime's feudal apparatus, was abolished and the palace later became the city's Law Court (Gerechthof), a role that it retained until 1984. Four years later the palace took on a new lease of life as Bruges City Council's administrative offices.

Below: Palace of the Liberty of Bruges

Meeting of minds
Charles V visited Bruges in 1515, the same year that England's Thomas More met the humanist Erasmus in the city, while on a diplomatic mission for King Henry VIII, beginning an intellectual association that influenced his *Utopia.*

Renaissance Hall

The four burgomasters and 28 aldermen of the Liberty met in the ★★ **Renaissance Hall of the Liberty of Bruges** (Renaissancezaal Brugse Vrije; open Tues–Sun 9.30am–12.30pm, 1.30–5pm; tickets also cover entry to the Gothic Hall). This magnificent hall in the palace has now been restored to its original condition, with the aldermen's benches and office-holders' *buffet* (table) in their correct positions, and adorned by big brass inkwells and heavy law books.

The room's black Dinant marble fireplace decorated with an alabaster frieze is surmounted by a superb carved oak chimneypiece. It dates from 1529 and is dedicated to the Holy Roman Emperor Charles V, who visited Bruges in 1515 at the age of 15.

The fireplace celebrates the imperial army's victory at Pavia over Francis I of France in 1525 – the Treaty of Madrid, which was signed the following year, broke Belgium free from French domination. Charles, with raised sceptre and the orb of empire in his hands, and sporting an impressive codpiece along with his armour, stands in the centre beneath the double-headed eagle emblem of the Habsburg Empire. He is flanked by his grandparents: Emperor Maximilian of Austria, Duchess Mary of Burgundy, King Ferdinand II of Aragon and Queen Isabella I of Castile.

Charles V carved in oak in the Renaissance Hall of the Liberty of Bruges

The four panels of the alabaster frieze depict the biblical tale of Suzanna being falsely accused by the Elders, who literally get their lumps in return by being stoned to death – a no doubt salutary tale for the lawmakers who used to meet here. Note the three brass handholds hanging from the mantelpiece: these were used by the aldermen to steady themselves while they dried their boots at the fire.

Civic Registry

Between the years of 1534 and 1537, the Flemish Renaissance-style ★ **Civic Registry** (Burgerlijke Griffie) ❷ was built adjacent to the palace as the offices of the Town Clerk, and were later used by the court recorder. It has the oldest surviving Renaissance facade in the city, although with Gothic elements, and is still used to house the Municipal Archives. Its three scrolled gables are particularly fine. The building has recently been restored to bring out the original colours on the facade.

★

Star Attractions
- **Renaissance Hall of the Liberty of Bruges**
- **Town Hall**

GOTHIC TOWN HALL

To its right is the graceful, triple-turreted Gothic ★★★ **Town Hall** (Stadhuis) ❸. This refined-looking late 14th-century building actually began life as a prison, and is the oldest Town Hall in Belgium. It resembles nothing so much as a large stone copy of one of the ornate reliquaries you often see in Flemish churches.

Its magnificent ★ **Gothic Hall** (Gotische Zaal) upstairs (open Tues–Sun 9.30am–5pm) is particularly worth seeing for its vaulted carved-oak ceiling and biblical murals dating from 1385 to 1402. There are also some less notable but nonetheless very interesting 19th-century murals, portraying events in the city's history, in addition to an engraved Map of Bruges produced by Marcus Gerards in 1562.

Restored and cleaned up in the 1980s, the Town Hall has a pristine look which extends to the statues in the niches on the facade. These are 1980s' replacements for the original biblical and histor-

Below: the Civic Registry and the Town Hall
Bottom: part of a 19th-century mural in the Gothic Hall

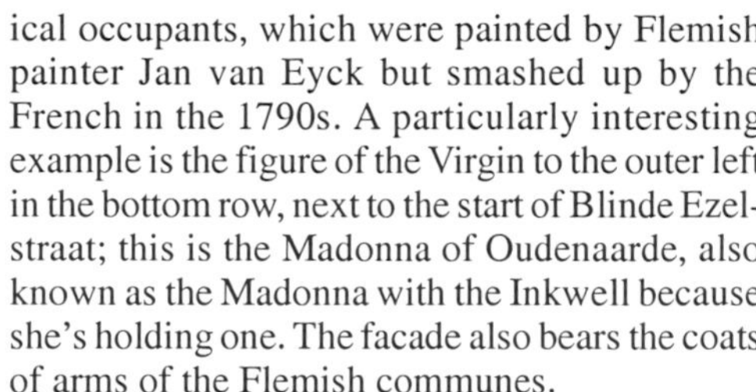

ical occupants, which were painted by Flemish painter Jan van Eyck but smashed up by the French in the 1790s. A particularly interesting example is the figure of the Virgin to the outer left in the bottom row, next to the start of Blinde Ezelstraat; this is the Madonna of Oudenaarde, also known as the Madonna with the Inkwell because she's holding one. The facade also bears the coats of arms of the Flemish communes.

Below: inside St Basil's Chapel
Bottom: altar in the Basilica of the Holy Blood

BASILICA OF THE HOLY BLOOD

Continuing clockwise around the square, you come next to the ★★★ **Basilica of the Holy Blood** (Heilig-Bloedbasiliek) ❹ (open Apr–Sept: daily 9.30am–noon and 2–6pm; Oct–Mar: 10am– noon and 2–4pm; closed Wed pm). On the ground floor of the basilica is the Romanesque **St Basil's Chapel** (Sint-Basiliuskapel). Built from 1139 to 1149 as the church of the now vanished Castle of the Counts, it has a tympanum with a bas-relief of the baptism of Christ.

RELIC OF THE HOLY BLOOD

The upper floor, reached by a spiral staircase, was remodelled in Gothic style in the 15th century, and houses a venerated **Relic of the Holy Blood**. This scrap of cloth, stained with what is said to be the blood of Christ washed from his body by

Joseph of Arimathaea, is kept inside a rock-crystal phial and is supposed to have been brought to Bruges from Jerusalem in 1150 by Count Thierry of Alsace (Diederik van de Elzas), who received it for bravery during the Second Crusade. An alternative and perhaps more likely explanation is that it was brought from Constantinople in the time of Count Baldwin IX, who served as the first, and short-lived, Latin Emperor of Constantinople from 1204 to 1205, after the Fourth Crusade had taken the Byzantine capital by storm and looted its treasures and relics. The relic can be seen, and kissed if you so desire. It is carried through the city on Ascension Day in the Procession of the Holy Blood *(see page 103)*.

Also in the church is the ★ **Relic Museum** (same opening hours as the basilica), where the magnificent gold and silver reliquaries in which the phial is kept can be seen. In addition, there are religious items and some triptych panels by Peter Pourbus that illustrate the Brotherhood of the Holy Blood.

If all this architectural history has left you in need of refreshment, relief is immediately at hand at the traditional Flemish **Brasserie Tom Pouce**, occupying the row of gabled houses to the right of the basilica (actually it is to the right of a small modern shopping arcade that would do the Burg a very big favour by disappearing).

THE PROVOST'S HOUSE

There is, however, one more monumentally interesting building to look at before you leave the Burg: the ornately decorated **Provost's House** (Proosdij) ❺, rebuilt in baroque style from 1665–6 on the earlier residence of the Dean of the Romanesque **St Donatian's Church** (Sint-Donaaskerk), which used to stand next door. The Proosdij became the seat of the Bishop of Bruges when the post was created in 1559. But in fact the first Bishop was not installed until 1562, when he also took over as Dean of St Donatian's, which subsequently became a cathedral. The house later passed to the provincial governor, and is now

Star Attraction

• **Basilica of the Holy Blood**

Prized relic

The main reliquary in the Basilica of the Holy Blood's Relic Museum – the one used during the Procession of the Holy Blood – was made by Bruges goldsmith Jan Crabbe in 1617. One of its most valuable components is a diamond that is supposed to have belonged to Queen Mary Stuart of Scotland; the crown on top of it belonged to Duchess Mary of Burgundy.

Below: Brasserie Tom Pouce
Bottom: Provost's House

occupied by West Flanders Province's press and public relations department.

FROM CHURCH TO HOTEL

St Donatian's was believed to have been built in around 950, and it was here that the Count of Flanders Charles the Good was murdered in 1127 while at prayer, and the painter Jan van Eyck was buried in the church in 1441. However, it eventually bit the dust around 1800 courtesy of the anti-clerical French who then occupied Bruges.

All that remains of the Carolingian-style cathedral's original choir gallery has been excavated and incorporated into the cellars of the **Crowne Plaza Brugge Hotel** *(see page 116)*, a late 20th-century, post-modern deluxe hotel designed to do as little visual damage to the ancient square as possible.

Facing the hotel, a starkly modern pavilion stands on the site of the vanished cathedral. Designed by the Japanese architect Toyo Ito, it is one of several new buildings that were commissioned by the city during its year as European capital of culture. The aim of these projects was to prove that Bruges was a dynamic city, not just a preserved Medieval town, though most tourists are attracted by its historic monuments.

You can make a brief detour past the hotel into adjacent Hoogstraat, to the crumbling Huis van de Zeven Torens (House of the Seven Towers), at No. 7, which dates from 1320 and is currently being restored. It might more appropriately be called the House Without Seven Towers, as it has been shorn of them all.

Below: Crowne Plaza Brugge Hotel
Bottom: The Lovers

TO THE MARKT

Almost lost among the plane trees at the edge of the square, look for the tender modern sculpture of *The Lovers*. This represents the starry-eyed couples who get married at the Town Hall opposite and, as often as not, start married life in one of the horse-drawn carriages that come trundling in from the nearby Markt.

And that's where we're heading next, backtracking past the Proosdij and taking the short Breidelstraat, past **Breydel-De Coninck** at No. 24, an excellent restaurant specialising in mussels, to emerge into Bruges' second historic square, the ★★★ **Markt.** In most Flemish and Dutch towns, the main square is called the Grote Markt (Great Square), but Bruges' has no need of such an adjectival booster. It is certainly one of the most perfectly laid out squares in the country, even if, under the great commercial pressure that goes with Bruges' success in attracting tourists, most of its gabled houses have been turned into restaurants. Should you want to have lunch or dinner in the Markt, La Civière d'Or at No. 33, in the former Fishmongers' Guildhouse, is a good place to choose.

Star Attractions
- Markt
- The Belfry

Giddy up
Horse-and-carriage tours leave from the Markt all day and every day except during the Wednesday street market, when the carriages redeploy to the Burg.

Below: ticket to ride
Bottom: gabled houses

THE BELFRY

With heraldic banners floating from its facade, the Markt is dominated by the enormous ★★★ **Belfry** (Belfort) ❻ (open Tues–Sun 9.30am–5pm). Rising 84m (275ft) above the square, the Belfry is one of the landmarks, together with the towers of Holy Saviour's Cathedral *(see page 42)* and the Church of Our Lady *(page 37)*, that makes the city visible from far away across the Flanders countryside.

A wooden spire once crowned the Belfry, as you can see in old prints such as Marcus Gerards'

1562 *Map of Bruges*, but it burned down in 1493 and the same fate befell a replacement in 1741, leaving the tower, tall as it is, with a truncated look. Be that as it may, the Belfry tilts 1.2m (4ft) from the vertical at its summit – any votes for the Leaning Tower of Bruges?

The lower section of the tower dates from around 1240, with the corner turrets added in the 14th century and the upper, octagonal section in the 15th century. This was the city treasury in medieval times, and a highly visible symbol of Bruges' wealth and importance. The aldermen used to meet in a chamber here until a fire in 1280 drove them away to their present location in the Burg. If you have the stamina, you can climb its winding staircase of 366 steps, past the second-floor treasury (where the town seal and charters were kept safely and securely behind multiple wrought-iron grilles), on to the impressive clock mechanism, and finally to a fantastic and windy panoramic view of Bruges and the surrounding countryside all the way to the sea.

The 47-bell carillon is served by a full-time *carilloneur*, and when you stand here the pealing of the bells every 15 minutes can be nearly deafening. Better to hear them from further away while sitting on one of the Markt's café terraces, or in the Market Halls courtyard, especially for the longer concerts that take place several times

Below: The Belfry
Bottom: Provincial House

a week in summer (mid-June–Sept: Mon, Wed and Sat 9–10pm, Sun 2.15–3pm; Oct–mid-June: Wed, Sat and Sun 2.15–3pm).

Star Attraction
• **Market Halls**

THE MARKET HALLS

Below and around the Belfry, forming a complex of awesome proportions, is the ★★ **Market Halls** (Hallen) ❼. This dates principally from 1240 to the 15th century, with later additions made due to fire, and it replaced an earlier wooden structure on the same site. Formerly used by merchants and for fairs, it was for three centuries the pride of the city, and the focal point of its commercial life. Recently it has come back into use as a commercial and exhibition centre, operated by the Adornes consortium of local art dealers.

If you pass through the arched entranceway to the interior courtyard, you will find yourself surrounded by galleries. In front of the Market Halls is a bronze replica of the Belfry and Market Halls together, with Braille inscriptions.

Local lads made good
Both Jan Breydel and Pieter De Coninck did very nicely out of their rebel stand against the French in 1302. Breydel became one of the city's wealthiest citizens and remained active in local politics. De Coninck was knighted. Since there were plenty of vacant houses in town that had belonged to French sympathisers, now dead or departed, they each picked themselves out a fine one and moved in.

PROVINCIAL HOUSE

In neo-Gothic style and almost as equally ornate as the Belfry and Market Halls, the ★ **Provincial House** (Provincaal Hof) ❽ is situated on the adjacent side of the Markt after the main Post Office as you go around anti-clockwise.

Dating principally from 1887 to 1892, it is today the government building of West Flanders Province and the seat of the Provincial Governor, who represents both the Royal Court and the Federal Government in Brussels.

Sculpture group with Jan Breydel and Pieter de Coninck

LOCAL HEROES

The **sculpture group** ❾ in the centre of the Markt was completed in 1887 and depicts two popular if unlikely local heroes: the butcher Jan Breydel and the weaver Pieter de Coninck. In 1302 they led a rebellion against the occupying French, and helped the ragtag Flemish rebels to annihilate an army of heavily armoured French knights at the

The golden spurs
After a battle on the Groeninge plain near Kortrijk (Courtrai) on 11 July, 1302 in which the Flemish rebels beat the armoured French, 700 golden spurs were collected from the field. Hence the battle has gone down in history as the Battle of the Golden Spurs. Philip the Fair eventually yielded to the rebels' demands and granted Flanders its independence.

The Craenenburg

Battle of the Golden Spurs later that same year. During the statue's unveiling in 1887, King Leopold II and the city's mayor stirred up understandable local outrage by addressing in French the crowd of people who had come to honour their historic, French-battling Flemish heroes.

THE CRAENENBURG

On the corner of Markt and Sint-Amandstraat is a turreted and crenellated mansion, the **Craenenburg** ⑩. Now a restaurant, in the Middle Ages it was a residence for the Count's knights and their ladyfolk. In 1482 the citizens imprisoned Crown Prince Maximilian of Austria here for 100 days, after the Habsburg authorities had imposed new taxes.

The audacity of locking up the Crown Prince of the House of Habsburg, who was later to become Emperor Maximilian I and known as the 'last knight', caused a stir across Europe. His father, Emperor Frederick III, dispatched warships and Maximilian was set free, but not before his counsellor, Pieter Lanchals, had been beheaded and Maximilian had been forced to make a pledge to respect the rights of the touchy burghers of Bruges. No sooner had he been released than he went back on his word, exacting revenge by moving the ducal residence to Ghent and transferring its commercial privileges to Antwerp, thereby undermining Bruges' importance. He also obliged the citizens to keep swans in the canals for ever (Lanchals' family emblem was a swan); as you can see, Bruges is still, and enthusiastically, paying off this part of its debt.

DE BOUCHOUTE

Opposite the Craenenburg is the medieval mansion **De Bouchoute**, where the exiled English King Charles II stayed in 1656–57. Dating from 1480, it was restored in 1995 to its original brick Gothic condition. The octagonal compass and weathervane (1682) on the roof allowed merchants to judge their ships' chances of entering or leaving port.

2: Along the Central Canal

Fish Market – De Pelikaan – Huidenvettersplein – Rozenhoedkaai – Dijver – Groeninge Museum – Brangwyn Museum – Gruuthuse Museum – Church of Our Lady – Guido Gezelleplein

Beginning in the heart of Bruges, in the Burg, this route follows the old waterways of the Rivers Dijver and Reie, now a canal, taking in some of the city's stellar museums and religious sites along the way. It should leave a powerful impression of Bruges' cultural and historical wealth, not to mention the city's bustling present.

Below: Blind Donkey Street
Bottom: Fish market sign

THE FISH MARKET

One of the nice things about starting this route in the Burg is walking through **Blind Donkey Street** (Blinde Ezelstraat) – the origin of this name, as you might expect, is obscure – a narrow passageway that begins with a vaulted arcade between the Town Hall and the Oude Griffie, and brings you to the bridge over the canal at Steenhouwersdijk. On your right is a jetty for the half-hour canal-boat tours of Bruges, one of which you ought to take at some point *(see page 113)*.

After crossing the bridge, to your left stands the colonnaded arcade of the ★ **Fish Market** (Vismarkt) ⓫, completed in 1821. Here, on mornings

Eating on the square
While in Huidenvettersplein, you may also want to check out the **Duc de Bourgogne** at No 12, one of the city's most characterful restaurants, serving French-style food in beautiful surroundings. **'t Mozarthuys** at No 1 is another good bet.

from Tuesday to Saturday, you can treat yourself to the sight of fresh fish from the North Sea ports being sliced and, in the case of *haring* (herring), often being popped raw into the mouths of the nearest humans. At weekends there is also a small crafts market here, an outpost of the market that occupies the nearby Dijver *(see opposite)*. The Fish Market is one of the few notable structures bequeathed by the period of Dutch rule from 1815 to 1830.

Continue by the water, past the Die Swaene hotel. Across the canal, you can see elements of the early 16th-century **Palace of the Liberty of Bruges** *(see page 21)* that were unaffected by the rebuilding of 1722–7. The baroque mansion that stands beside the water next to it is De Caese, which formed part of the Liberty of Bruges complex until 1988, when it was sold to and restored by the Paribas Bank.

De Pelikaan

De Pelikaan Almshouse

Keep going into Groenerei past two old stone bridges, the Meebrug and the Peerdenbrug, to the end of the wharf. At the corner is a house called **De Pelikaan** ⓬, which used to be an almshouse and hospital for the poor; it dates from 1714 and is decorated with a pelican emblem over the doorway. Almshouses, of which there are several examples in Bruges dating from the 15th to the 18th centuries, were built by wealthy individuals and trade guilds as refuges for the old and the poor *(see page 47)*.

Retrace your steps along Groenerei and Steenhouwersdijk to magical **Huidenvettersplein** ⓭, where the tanners used to have their guildhouse – the **Ambachtshuis der Huidevetters** – dating from 1630–31, and now housing the upscale 't Huidevettershuis restaurant. These days, summer tourists on the square's café terraces tan their own hides while street artists record the scene for posterity. Note the small column topped by two lions. At the end of the square, turn briefly left to 7 Braambergstraat for a look at De Kogge, an antique tavern in the former Fish Porters' Guildhouse from 1637.

VIEW FROM ROZENHOEDKAAI

If for some reason you feel that Bruges hasn't yet lived up to its picturesque reputation, you will certainly revise your opinion as soon as you emerge on to **Rozenhoedkaai** ⓮. The ★★★ **view** over the canal is stunning, following the line of the River Dijver, the old waterside houses and the Belfry. Taking a break here at the corner café 't Klein Venetië (Little Venice) is maybe a little obvious, but the outlook makes up for the lack of adventure. Winston Churchill is one of the many artists, amateur and professional, who have painted the scene from Rozenhoedkaai.

Star Attraction
- **view from Rozenhoedkaai**

Below: Statue of St John of Nepomucene
Bottom: view from Rozenhoedkaai

THE DIJVER

In front of you is a bridge, the **Sint-Jan Nepomucenusbrug**, named after the Czech martyr John of Nepomuk. He is patron saint of bridges – having been pitched, in 1393, from the Charles Bridge in Prague into the Vltava River for opposing King Wenceslas's attempts to create a new bishopric for one of his favourites (or as legend would have it, for refusing to reveal the confessions of the queen) – and his statue, dating from 1767, stands between two wrought-iron lamps on the bridge.

Keep walking along the canal to the **Dijver** ⓯, a tree-shaded bank where the weekend antiques

and flea market is held from March to October. Across the water is the rear end of the former **Carthusian Convent**, and the orangery at the back of the 19th-century **De Halleux House** in Oude Burg *(see page 41)*. On this side, the house at No. 7 still has windowpanes made of Venetian glass, and at No. 11 you will see the Europa College, a postgraduate centre for Euro-studies.

Flemish primitives
The hallmarks of Flemish Primitive art are clarity and realism, an acute sense of light, robustly naturalistic native backgrounds, and a gift for portrayal. The artists' patient powers of observation ensured an accurate portrayal of the texture of cloth, the warmth of flesh, and the vivid surfaces of life. Where the Florentines excelled at perspective and foreshortening, the Flemish relied on amassing detail upon detail.

Groeninge Museum

Next door at No. 12, a pathway leads to the Municipal Fine Arts Museum (Stedelijk Museum voor Schone Kunsten), more commonly known as the ★★★**Groeninge Museum** ⓰ (open Tues–Sun 9.30am–5pm). The gallery is small in terms both of its physical size and the size of its collection, yet in terms of the quality of what you can see here, it certainly deserves to be ranked among the world's great museums.

Groeninge Museum entrance

Built in 1930 on the site of a former Augustinian monastery, it houses a superb collection of works by the so-called 'Flemish Primitives' of the 15th century. Far from being primitive, these painters were responsible for a revolutionary step forward in art, moving away from rigidly religious medieval themes and portraying real people.

Works on display include Jan van Eyck's *Madonna and Child with Canon Joris van der Paele, St Donatian and St John,* and *Portrait of Margareta van Eyck* (his wife); Hans Memling's *Moreel Triptych;* Hugo van der Goes' *Death of the Virgin;* and works by Rogier van der Weyden, Pieter Pourbus, Gerard David and others *(see Art, pages 97–100)*.

A nonchalantly gruesome work hanging in the museum is the *Judgement of Cambyses* (1498) by Gerard David, showing a corrupt Persian judge being flayed alive by some industrious torturers. Another important painting is *The Last Judgement* by Hieronymous Bosch, a grim but complicated account of the trials that await sinners in the after-life. Also, don't ignore less advertised paintings such as *The Town Docks at Bruges* (1653) by Hendrik van Minderhout, which gives an idea of the size of the merchant ships that routinely called at Bruges. There are also modern works by Magritte, Delvaux, the Flemish Expressionists and others to be seen.

The museum was recently renovated, and paintings are now hung in a bold new style. Some rooms have walls crowded with paintings, while others have works hung on metal racks or even attached to the ceiling. Not all visitors are impressed at this radical transformation.

Star Attraction
• **Groeninge Museum**

Below: a portrait by Hans Memling.
Bottom: Horsemen of the Apocalypse

BRANGWYN AND LACE

Across the Arents Park at No. 16 is the ★ **Arents House** ⓱ (open Tues–Sun 9.30am–5pm). The museum is dedicated to the works of British artist Frank Brangwyn (1867–1956) who was, and still is, a big hit in Bruges, firstly because he was born here, and secondly because he came back here to paint here.

The oil paintings, watercolours and etchings Brangwyn bequeathed to the city are housed on the first floor of a late 18th-century mansion, the Hof Arents, while the ground floor is used for temporary exhibitions of prints and drawings.

In the garden, take a look at the modern sculptures of the **Four Horsemen of the Apocalypse**, which represent the horrors of war, death, famine and revolution.

Rich refuge
A fantastic Burgundian Gothic tracery of rose-coloured stone with high towers and arched windows (much of it 19th-century reconstruction), the Palace of the Lords of Gruuthuse was a refuge for the exiled English kings Edward IV in 1470–71 and Charles II in 1656.

GRUUTHUSE MUSEUM

The courtyard pathway beside the Brangwyn Museum leads across the narrow and pretty **Boniface Bridge** (Bonifatiusbrug) – note the tiny, timber-faced canalside houses to your left – and past a statue of the Spanish-born resident of Bruges, the humanist philosopher Juan Luis Vivés (1492–1540), whose writings led the authorities to introduce measures for the relief of the poor in the city.

You then come to the lavish 15th-century ★★ **Palace of the Lords of Gruuthuse** ⓲, built by a family who had a lucrative monopoly on the sale of *gruut* (a mixture of herbs for improving the flavour of beer), and later the tax concession on beer itself.

Its leading light was Lodewijk van Gruuthuse (*circa* 1427–92), who was a counsellor to the Burgundian dukes Philip the Good and Charles the Bold, and whose equestrian statue stands sentinel above the entrance.

Below: Gruuthuse Palace
Bottom: view from Boniface Bridge

DECORATIVE ARTS

Since 1955 the palace has been the **Gruuthuse Museum** (open Tues–Sun 9.30am–5pm), whose treasures of the decorative arts represent life – at least as it was lived by the high and mighty – in 15th- and 16th-century Bruges. There are 2,500 objects in the house, including paintings, sculp-

tures, musical instruments, lace, silk, tapestries, furniture, weapons and glassware. In one room is a bust of Emperor Charles V as an optimistic young man of 20 years old, crafted before the cares of war, religious strife and political intrigue had worn him to a frazzle.

You can kneel in Lodewijk van Gruuthuse's oak-panelled Gothic oratory, which dates from 1472. This is a private chapel that abuts the adjacent Church of Our Lady, and afforded Lodewijk and his family an undisturbed, overhead view of the altar and of the tombs of Duke Charles the Bold of Burgundy and his daughter Duchess Mary *(see page 38)*. The family's motto, *Plus Est En Vous* (There Is More In You), can be seen above an arch in the ornate reception hall.

The mansion's former stables in the courtyard now house a cafeteria, but the **Maria van Boergondië** restaurant at 1 Guido Gezelleplein is a more congenial place in which to recover from your exertions.

Star Attractions
- **Palace of the Lords of Gruuthuse**
- **Church of Our Lady**

CHURCH OF OUR LADY

Pass through the grove of lime trees, under the archway, and through a narrow alley to the ★★★ **Church of Our Lady** (Onze-Lieve-Vrouwekerk) ⓳ (open Tues–Sat 9.30am–12.30pm and 1.30–5pm, Sun 1.30–5pm).

Church of Our Lady

First mentioned in records in 1089, the church was by then already two centuries old. Its 122-m (400-ft) brick spire is an even more visible landmark than that of the Belfry in the Markt *(see pages 27–8)* – the tower of Antwerp Cathedral pips it at the post by just 1m (3ft) for the honour of tallest spire in the Low Countries.

It is inside the 13th–15th-century church, however, that its true glories lie. First among these is the ★★★ *Madonna and Child* by Michelangelo *(see picture on page 99)*. Originally sculpted in 1504 for the Cathedral of Siena, which couldn't afford to pay for it when it was completed, the statue was snapped up by the wealthy Bruges merchant Jan van Mouskroen and donated to the church in 1506. It was the only work by

Michelangelo to leave Italy during the artist's lifetime, and is still one of very few that can be seen outside his native country. The smallish Carrara marble sculpture, kept behind protective glass in a small side chapel, is spellbindingly beautiful, although its proportions have led some commentators to conclude that it was designed to be viewed from a lower angle than its present situation allows.

Below: stained glass
Bottom: tomb of Mary of Burgundy

THE ROYAL CHAPEL AND TOMBS

During the Burgundian period, Our Lady's was the Royal Chapel of the Dukes of Burgundy, and it was here in 1477 that Mary of Burgundy, daughter of Charles the Bold, married the Crown Prince of the Habsburg Empire, Maximilian of Austria, in a ceremony that was noted for its lavishness and for the fact that the bride and groom didn't speak the other's language.

Maximilian made a triumphal entry into the city for his wedding, his armour gleaming with silver gilt, a diadem of pearls and precious stones instead of a helmet atop his blond locks, and the black cross of Burgundy emblazoned on his breastplate.

In the church's choir you can see the magnificent side-by-side ★★ **tombs of Charles the Bold and Mary**. Charles was killed in 1477 at the Bat-

tle of Nancy (after his band of Italian mercenaries went over to the other side), and it was a riding accident that took Mary's life in 1482 at the age of just 25, no doubt to Maximilian's distress (although he may have felt compensated by inheriting his late wife's realm).

Mary's sarcophagus, made from black marble surmounted by a graceful, reclining image of her in bronze, dates from 1502 and is a superb work of late Gothic art. Her father's, also furnished with a recumbent image of the deceased in bronze – although there is some doubt about whether the remains inside are really those of Charles – was not completed until the mid-16th century. By that time the Renaissance style was in vogue, and it is interesting to compare the differences between the two today.

There are many other stately memorials in the church, including the **funerary chapel of Pieter Lanchals**, Maximilian of Austria's executed counsellor, with a painting of Our Lady of the Seven Sorrows by Adrian Isenbrandt from around 1520; a painting of the *Crucifixion* by Anthony van Dyck, as well as works by Dirk Bouts and Hugo van der Goes; and a complete set of escutcheons (shields bearing a coat of arms) of the Knights of the Golden Fleece, who held a chapter meeting in the Church of Our Lady in 1468.

STATUE OF GUIDO GEZELLE

Come out into the street that runs around the side of the church, Onze-Lieve-Vrouwekerkhof-Zuid, for a look at the pink Art Nouveau facade of the **house at Nos. 6–8**, built in 1904 and with murals of Day and Night painted over the doorways.

Continuing on and around brings you to Gruuthusestraat, and across that to **Guido Gezelleplein** ⓴. In this square stands a statue, erected in 1930, of the Bruges poet and priest Guido Gezelle (1830–99), who was one of the principal 19th-century Flemish men of letters, and founder of the Flemish Academy of Language and Literature *(see pages 58, 63, 101–102)*.

Star Attraction
• Tombs of Charles the Bold and Mary

Hiawatha
Fluent in English, the poet and priest Guido Gezelle translated several English works into Dutch, among them Henry Wadsworth Longfellow's epic American poem *The Song of Hiawatha* (1855).

Art Nouveau facade of house Nos. 6–8 in Onze-Lieve-Vrouwekerkhof-Zuid

3: To the Lake of Love

Carthusian Convent and Church – Hof van Watervliet – Simon Stevinplein – Holy Saviour's Cathedral – Archaeological Museum – St John's Hospital and Memling Museum – Halve Maan Brewery – Begijnhof – Lake of Love – Godshuis de Vos – Municipal Fine Arts Academy – De Meulenaere, St Joseph and Our Lady of the Seven Sorrows Almshouses

Beginning in the Markt square and passing through some busy shopping streets, this tour leads to several important religious and civic monuments. After pausing for appropriate refreshment at a famous Bruges brewery, producer of the strapping Straffe Hendrik brew, it culminates in the peace of the Begijnhof convent and the scenic Lake of Love.

Below: nun at the Beguinage
Bottom: Oude Burg

WOLLESTRAAT

Take the busy Wollestraat shopping street at the southeast corner of the Markt, beside the Market Halls. Follow it to its end, past the classic **'t Bourgoensche Cruyce** restaurant at Nos. 41–43 (an atmospheric old hotel with views over the canal and fine traditional regional Flemish cuisine, *see pages 106 and 117*), to just before the bridge over the Reie. Three reliefs on the facade

of the house at No. 28 show scenes from the 1631 siege of Bruges by the Protestant Dutch army of Prince Frederik Henry of Orange. On the left, at No. 53, stands the ornate **De Malvenda House**, which in the 16th century was the residence of the Spanish magistrate Juan Perez de Malvenda.

CARTHUSIAN MEMENTOES

Walk back a short way and turn left into the dog-legged Karthuizerinnenstraat, lined by the buildings that gave the street its name, the 16th–17th century former Carthusian Convent (Karthuizerinnen Klooster) and Carthusian Church (Karthuizerinnenkerk). The convent buildings are now offices of the local social services, and the church is a military chapel. The crypt contains the ashes of Dachau concentration camp victims, and on the walls are plaques bearing the names of the dead from both world wars.

Emerging through the archway into Oude Burg, straight ahead in the loggia of the lace shop at No. 4, a mannequin 'elderly woman' works unceasingly at her lace-making. Turn left along Oude Burg and then right into dead-end Oude Zomerstraat, where at No. 2 there is a townhouse dating from around 1500. If you return to Oude Burg and continue along it, in quick succession you will see three interesting houses. First is the **De Halleux House** at No. 21, a neoclassical townhouse built in the 19th century. This house has a more famous view, from across the Dijver to the 18th-century canalside orangery at the rear *(see page 34)*.

Next comes the **Hof van Watervliet** ㉒ at No. 27. It was built around 1450 as the home of Jan de Baenst, a leading light in Bruges, whose unswerving loyalty to the House of Burgundy earned him fame and fortune – and the enmity of his fellow citizens. It was at that time called the Hof van Sint-Joris, as de Baenst hailed from the district of Sint-Joris-ten-Distel outside the city. Then the mansion became home to Pieter Lanchals, Crown Prince Maximilian's pro-taxation *consigliere*, executed by unenthusiastic taxpayers

Art donor

Jan de Baenst, who lived at Hof van Watervliet, near the Carthusian Convent, seems to have been the donor of the *Legend of St Ursula* (*circa* 1482), a masterpiece by the anonymous Master of the St Ursula Legend, displayed in the Groeninge Museum *(see page 34)*. This incredibly detailed, eight-panel painting depicts the same legend of St Ursula and her 11,000 Virgins as does Hans Memling's famous shrine in the same museum. De Baenst is known to have been a patron of the convent which received the polyptych and historians believe he and his family appear in some of its scenes.

Making lace at No. 4 Oude Burg

Map on pages 18–19

in 1488 – ironically it now accommodates the Hof Lanchals health and welfare centre. Later the house was bought by the humanist Marc Laurin, who was Lord of Watervliet, and it was renamed after him. Finally, at **No. 33**, is a house with a Renaissance facade dating from 1571.

Brain drain

As a Protestant, Simon Stevin is a prime example of the kind of talent Bruges and other Flemish cities lost when the Spanish King Philip II sought to reimpose Catholicism throughout his empire by repression and armed force. Within the sanctuary of Holland, Stevin thought up the decimal system and the science of hydrostatics, and made advances in fields as diverse as astronomy, navigation, accounting and military engineering.

Simon Stevinplein

This brings you to ★ **Simon Stevinplein** ㉓, and its sculpture of Simon Stevin (1548–1620). The great Bruges mathematician and scientist fled from his native city around 1580 during the anti-Protestant persecutions carried out by its Spanish rulers, and went to live and work in Holland in the service of Prince Maurits of Nassau. The square was laid out in 1819 during Dutch rule and the bronze statue, which depicts Stevin holding a set of dividers in one hand and a manuscript in the other, dates from 1847.

The **Bhavani** restaurant at No. 5 in the square should appeal to devotees of Indian cuisine *(see page 106)*.

Simon Stevinplein

Holy Saviour's Cathedral

Turn left into Steenstraat to visit the richly decorated ★★ **Holy Saviour's Cathedral** (Sint-Salvatorskathedraal) ㉔, which is often described, erroneously, as having been founded by St Elegius in 646. In fact, this is the original parish church, Bruges' oldest, and dates from the 9th century, though the earliest written reference to it is in 988 in a papal bull of Pope John XV. The structure is now mainly Gothic in style (13th–16th century), having succumbed to several fires, but it still retains some surviving Romanesque elements. It has a 100-m (328-ft) brick belfry. In an antechamber directly beneath the belfry, activating the light will allow you to look up right inside the tower, providing a startling geometric effect.

When Bruges found itself a cathedral-free zone, after French occupation forces demolished St Donatian's Cathedral in the Burg, Holy Saviour's was pressed into service in 1834 as a replacement seat for the Bishop of Bruges. The 15th-century wooden choir stalls flanking the altar bear a complete set of escutcheons of the Knights of the Golden Fleece *(see page 51)*, who held a chapter meeting here in 1478. Other notable features are the baroque rood-screen surmounted by the sculpture *God the Father*, by Antwerp artist Artus Quellin, the elaborate pulpit and the 18th-century tapestries beside the altar.

The **Cathedral Museum** (open Sun–Fri 2–5pm) houses, among other items that used to be on display in the cathedral, the *Martyrdom of St Hippolytus* (*circa* 1468) – a triptych by Dieric Bouts, with a side panel by Hugo van der Goes, depicting the unfortunate holy man being pulled apart by four horses – as well as the Cathedral Treasury of gold and silver religious vessels, elaborate reliquaries and some vestments.

Star Attraction
- **Holy Saviour's Cathedral**

Below: sculpture outside Holy Saviour's Cathedral
Bottom: reliquary inside the cathedral

ARCHAEOLOGICAL MUSEUM

Come out into Sint-Salvatorskerkhof, and take Heilige-Geeststraat at the eastern end. At No. 4 is the **Episcopal Palace**, a 16th-century mansion that's the residence of the bishop of Bruges. Continue to No. 36a where this street joins Mariastraat, for the **Archaeological Museum** ㉕ (open Tues–Sun 9.30am–12.30pm and 1.30–5pm) which contains a small but interesting collection

of pottery, glass, leather, wood, stone figurines and tomb paintings.

Return to Mariastraat and continue along it to the former ★★ **St John's Hospital** (Sint-Janshospitaal) 26, which was a work-in-progress from the 12th to the 17th centuries. Three of its wards and the Romanesque tower were built in the early 1200s, and two more wards were added in the late 1300s. The huge complex inside the 13th-century facade, with grounds that are a restful place to stroll around, is now divided between an arts and congress centre, as well as an internet café. In the cloisters near the entrance there is an interesting 17th-century **apothecary**.

Below: the exterior of St John's Hospital
Bottom: the canal frontage

MEMLING MUSEUM

Pride of place, however, goes to the ★★★ **Memling Museum** in the hospital's church (open Tues–Sun 9.30am–5pm). Here you can see the greatest works of the German-born painter Hans Memling (*circa* 1440–1494), who lived in Bruges from 1465 until his death (*see pages 98–9*). These include the *Mystic Triptych of St John,* part of an altarpiece that has side-panel images of John the Baptist and John the Evangelist; the *Adoration of the Magi,* notable for its serene image of the Virgin Mary; and the wooden *Shrine of St Ursula,* a reliquary in the shape of a Gothic

church, on whose panels Memling painted several scenes from the life of St Ursula, including her martyrdom by the Huns at Cologne (along with a reputed 11,000 virgins who had set out with her on a pilgrimage to Rome).

Star Attractions
- **St John's Hospital**
- **Memling Museum**
- **Begijnhof**

FINE VIEWS

Then, back on Mariastraat, turn right. A bridge over the canal provides splendid ★ **views** of the St John's Hospital frontage on one side and the shady canal on the other; steps lead down to a landing stage where canal cruises depart.

Over the bridge, on the right-hand side of the street, is an entrance to the **Spanoghe Almshouse**, dating from 1680. Turn right into the narrow lane called **Stoofstraat**, once home to a mixed public bath-house that basked in a steamy reputation, until it was closed when the authorities decided the proverbial proximity of cleanliness and godliness was no longer apparent.

Daring sculpture
Also in Walplein is a jaunty modern sculpture showing Leda and Zeus being whisked along in a carriage by the winged horse Pegasus. It could be considered somewhat sexist, if not downright prurient, as the naked Leda is splayed across the back seat and we all know what lecherous old Zeus had in mind, despite his cheerful wave.

HALVE MAAN BREWERY

The same could not be said of the ★**Halve Maan Brewery** ㉗ (guided visits Apr–Sept: daily every hour 11am–4pm; Oct–Mar: daily 11am–3pm) at Walplein 26, which was mentioned in dispatches as early as 1546. Today's foundation dates from the 19th century and produces Bruges' famous Straffe Hendrik beer, a strapping blond brew that can be sampled in the brewery's own brasserie – it is indeed a clean, heavenly taste.

Halve Maan Brewery sign

THE BEGIJNHOF

Spirituality of a more traditional kind is very much in evidence a short way off. If you head across Walplein, into Wijngaardstraat, then over the bridge that spans the Reie and through the 1776 neoclassical gateway, you will arrive at the Begijnhof, or in full the ★★★ **Princely Beguinage of the Vineyard** (Prinselijk Begijnhof ten Wijngaarde) ㉘, which gets its royal title from the fact that in 1299 France's King Philip IV placed it

In the Beguining
A Liège priest called Lambert de Bègue is said to have begun the Beguines, founding the first Béguinage in his city in 1189. The movement seems to have spread rapidly, reflecting both a lack of respectable ways for women to earn a livelihood at the time, and a shortage of men as the Crusades and other wars killed them off.

Beguinage entrance detail

under his patronage. Founded in 1245 (although most of its present buildings date from the 17th century) by the Countess of Flanders, Margaret of Constantinople, this tranquil refuge continued into this century as a home for *begijns* – religious women similar to nuns, except that they took no vows but lived an industrious, pious life caring for the sick and making lace. Since 1927, when they died out, the Begijnhof has been a Benedictine convent, upholding many of the traditions.

17TH-CENTURY COTTAGE

You can visit the Begijnhof's church, **Our Lady of Consolation of Spermalie** (Onze-Lieve-Vrouw van Troost van Spermalie), when the nuns are having a service. Or you can gain a glimpse of what their life must have been like at the **Begijnhuisje**, one of the *begijns*' small whitewashed cottages (open Apr–Sept: Mon–Sat 10am–noon and 2–5pm, Sun 10.30am–noon; Oct–Mar: Mon–Sat 10.30am–noon and 2–4pm, Sun 10.30am–noon), which is still essentially in its 17th-century condition. You can stroll around the cloister's large central garden, whose lawn is rich in poplar trees and is a blaze of colour in spring and summer.

LAKE OF LOVE

Leaving the Begijnhof by its south exit and turning left to the bridge, you see the old Lockkeeper's House (Sashuis) overlooking a long rectangular basin called the ★★ **Lake of Love** (Minnewater) ㉙. Its name seems to be a mistranslation – though a charming one – of an earlier name for this stretch of water, which once served as an interior port, the Binnenwater, where as many as 150 seagoing ships and canal barges loaded and unloaded cargo daily, during the city's 13th-century trading heyday as a member of the Hanseatic League. But it is nevertheless a truly idyllic and romantic spot, and you can stroll along the Minnewater's western bank – past public toilets whose presence might prove fortuitous.

On the other bank is the leafy ★**Minnewater Park** in which stands **Minnewater Castle** (Kasteel Minnewater), a château-style restaurant noted for its fine, relatively inexpensive food and a scenic waterside terrace.

Star Attraction
• Lake of Love

GODSHUIS DE VOS ALMSHOUSE

You may be happy to call it a day at this point and put your feet up at a café terrace, but if you're ready for more sightseeing on the way back to the centre, you can return there by a slightly different route. Take Wijngaardstraat and turn right into Noordstraat, to the ★**Godshuis de Vos Almshouse** ㉚ on the right-hand side of the street. Dating from 1713, this is a fine example of the Houses of God, or almshouses – tiny whitewashed houses built around a chapel, and generally tucked away from the world's prying eyes by a surrounding wall – that dot Bruges' streets.

The motivation for building these refuges for poor people and widows was a composite of religious duty, guilty conscience and insurance against popular unrest. In return, the grateful occupants prayed twice daily for their benefactor's soul in the chapel. Many almshouses are now owned by the city's social services department and continue to fulfil a similar role, with the possible exception of prayers for the director of

Below: Godshuis de Vos Almshouse
Bottom: Lake of Love and the lock-keeper's house

Best friends

Diamond polishing was one of the few industries in Bruges to show any signs of life during the hard economic times that followed World War I. Firms from Antwerp were attracted by the low wages paid to Bruges craftsmen.

Below: Fine Arts Academy, with a statue of Jan Van Eyck

social services. You can see over the wall into the courtyard garden of the Godshuis de Vos, with its original eight, now converted to six, little houses – and an enchanting sight it is.

Municipal Fine Arts Academy

Further along the street is a restored 16th-century chimney-tower and oven vault. From there, if you turn left into Arsenalstraat and left again into Katelijnestraat, you come to the **Municipal Fine Arts Academy** ㉛ (Stedelijk Academie voor Schone Kunsten) at No. 86. This is housed in the former community of the Beghards, male equivalents of the *begijns*, who set up shop here in the 13th century. The complex became a school for poor children in 1513 and took up its present academic duties in 1891.

Diamond Museum

Also in Katelijnestraat, at No. 43b, is the ★**Diamond Museum** (Diamantmuseum) ㉜ (open daily 10.30am–5.30pm). This museum in a building from 1634 focuses on the history of diamond polishing in Bruges. The technique of polishing diamonds using diamond powder on a rotating disk may have been invented by a Bruges goldsmith, Lodewijk van Berquen, around 1476, and processing diamonds has been an intermittently important industry in the city over the centuries. There are demonstrations of polishing, and tools and equipment on display.

More Almshouses

Continue up Katalijnestraat to its junction with Nieuwe Gentweg and turn right. Here in quick succession you can see the **De Meulenaere Almshouse** ㉝ at Nos. 12–22, dating from 1613; the **St Joseph Almshouse** (Sint-Jozef) at Nos. 24–32, dating from 1674; and the **Our Lady of the Seven Sorrows Almshouse** (Onze-Lieve-Vrouw van de Zeven Weeën) around the corner at Nos. 2–8 Drie Kroezenstraat, dating from 1654.

4: Out West

Statue of Flandria Nostra – Prince's Court (Prinsenhof) – Hof Sebrechts Park – Minstrel's Chapel – Church of Our Lady of the Blind – Marshal's Gate – Old Water House – Dumery Bell – St Godelieve Abbey – Capuchin Church – Van Campen, Van Peenen, Gloribus and Sucx Almshouses – 't Zand

This route moves away from the main sights and monuments of the historic centre and potters around among the mainly residential, shopping and religious edifices to the west of the Markt. It does, however, take in one of Bruges' most stellar buildings (the Prince's Court or Prinsenhof) as well as several stretches of greenery, before fetching up in the busy market square of 't Zand. A detour via a cluster of tradesmen's guildhouses takes you back to the Markt.

Muntplein

Leave the Markt by Sint-Amandstraat, between the medieval mansions called the **Craenenburg** and **De Bouchoute** *(see page 30)*, and at the end turn right into Geldmuntstraat, then left via Muntpoort to a little square called **Muntplein**. The names Muntplein and Geldmuntstraat – a *munt* is a mint, and *geld* is money – recall the coin mint

Below and bottom: De Moor Almshouse and detail

that once stood in adjacent Geerwijnstraat. In the square is a small **equestrian statue** ㉞ of Duchess Mary of Burgundy, known as Flandria Nostra. The daughter of Charles the Bold, she died in 1482 at age 25 after falling from her horse while hunting, and now occupies a magnificent sarcophagus in the Church of Our Lady *(see page 37)*. An equestrian statue might not seem entirely appropriate in the circumstances, but there she is, riding side-saddle on a horse that's pawing the air.

Below: Flandria Nostra on Muntplein
Bottom: De Medici Sorbetière

THE PRINSENHOF

Across the way, at No. 9, is the Art Nouveau shopfront of the **De Medici Sorbetière**, whose cakes and other confections also display a fanciful style and taste.

Continue west on Geldmuntstraat for a short way, and turn right at the next street, Prinsenhof. This is so called after the ★**Prince's Court** (Prinsenhof) ㉟, once the residence of the Dukes and Duchesses of Burgundy and the Habsburg Emperors and Empresses. During the Burgundian period this palace was the last word in pomp and splendour. Some considered it the last genuinely princely court of the Middle Ages. When Duke Charles the Bold was engaged in his ill-starred quest to secure a royal crown, and put Burgundy

right up there as the third continental power alongside France and Germany, the Prinsenhof was a radiant nucleus, and Bruges, his capital, the largest, richest and most powerful mercantile city north of the Alps.

So why is it worth only a measly one star? Because not much survived of the original 14th-century palace after the Revolutionary French took up residence in Bruges in 1794 and spent 20 years knocking down churches, monasteries and palaces (in their defence, most of the people of Bruges had become so disenchanted with the corrupt clerics and aristos beholden to the Austrian *ancien régime* that they often gave enthusiastic assistance to the demolition effort). In its original form, the palace would have been surrounded by high walls and battlements and stretched between Noordzandstraat and the parallel Moerstraat.

Some of the highlights of the Burgundian era took place in this setting. Duke Philip the Good celebrated his marriage to Isabella of Portugal in 1430, and Duke Charles the Bold his marriage to Margaret of York in 1468, with the kind of banquets that have made the term 'Burgundian' a symbol of lavishness taken to excess. Duchess Mary gave birth to Philip the Handsome here in 1479. In 1482, she died here, as did Philip the Good in 1467.

The marks of repairs and additions to the early structures that remain can be clearly seen as you walk through the ornamental gateway. Yet, though little of the original is there, the Prinsenhof is still an imposing place, having had a long and colourful history.

Golden fleece

The august Order of the Golden Fleece was founded by Duke Philip the Good in 1430 on the occasion of his marriage to Isabella of Portugal, and its knights formed the *crème de la crème* of Burgundian high society. But according to a no-doubt scurrilous French report published in 1620, the Golden Fleece referred not to the mythological quest of Jason and the Argonauts, but to the colour of the hair (in some accounts the pubic hair) of one of Philip the not-quite-so-Good's mistresses.

The Prinsenhof

MANY OWNERS

Remodelled constantly through the Burgundian century, the palace was put up for sale in 1631 by the cash-strapped Habsburgs, and bought in 1662 by the Order of St Francis to convert into a convent. In 1794, the nuns forestalled the incoming French demolition experts by departing for Delft and the property was sold again, after which

municipal housing was built on part of its extensive grounds. In 1888, nuns were back in residence, this time the sisters of the French Dames de la Retraite order. A century later it was sold to a private concern and used until recently for exhibitions, conferences and concerts. It has now been developed as a princely hotel-guesthouse, while retaining a cultural role.

Below: part of Minstrel's Chapel
Bottom: almshouses at Our Lady of the Blind

HOF SEBRECHTS PARK

Continue around into Ontvangersstraat, then left into Moerstraat, and across the canal into Beenhouwersstraat. The park here is the **Hof Sebrechts** ㊱, one of several oases in the city that owe their existence to the French demolition of the monasteries or convents that used to occupy them (in this case St Elisabeth's Convent). In the summer the park becomes an open-air museum for often weird and occasionally wonderful works of modern sculpture. Come back out into Moerstraat, and right to Speelmansrei, where on the corner stands the **Minstrel's Chapel** (Speelmanskapel) ㊲, dating from 1421.

CHURCH OF OUR LADY OF THE BLIND

As you reach the end of Speelmansrei, try to ignore the big, bustling, interesting-looking square dead ahead – it's the 't Zand. You'll be coming back to it shortly *(see page 54)*. Instead, turn right along Smedenstraat for four blocks, then right into Kreupelenstraat, to the church of ★**Our Lady of the Blind** (Onze-Lieve-Vrouw van Blindekens) ㊳. This bright and simple 17th-century church has a carved pulpit from 1659 and, most notably, a gilded 14th-century statue of the *Madonna and Child* above a side altar to the right of the main one.

Every 15 August, on the feast of the Assumption of the Virgin, a procession leaves from here and wends its way to the church of Our Lady of the Pottery (Onze-Lieve-Vrouw van de Potterie) in the northeast of the city *(see page 69)*.

MARSHAL'S GATE

Around the church, on Kreupelenstraat and Kammakersstraat, is a cluster of whitewashed almshouses, which provide an interesting diversion: the **Van Pamel**, **Marius Voet** and **Laurentia Soutieu Almshouses**.

Continuing along to the end of Smedenstraat brings you to the ★**Marshal's Gate** (Smedenpoort) ㊴, a fortified city gate. It is one of four that survive out of nine city gates that were once dotted around the now mostly vanished city walls. Dating from 1367–8, with additions from the 17th century, it is a powerful-looking lump of military stonework, giving some idea of the strength of Bruges' former moated defences, though the park that has replaced them is more agreeable to the eye.

Walls end

Maritime trade and textiles manufacture brought prosperity to the growing town during the 13th and 14th centuries, protected by walls thrown up around the inner canal circuit in the aftermath of Charles the Good's assassination in 1127. A second line of walls, punctuated by nine city gates, whose outline is preserved in the ring canal and its park *(see pages 77–80)*, was built during the 14th century. However, between 1782–4 the city walls were dismantled at the orders of the Austrian emperor. Many of the monasteries were closed then, too.

DUMERY BELL

If you walk south along the pathway through the park in the direction of Bruges station for about 110m (120yds), you come to the **Old Water House** (Oud Waterhuis) ㊵. This is an 18th-century construction that was part of the city's water-distribution system, drawing supplies from the canals and other sources.

Come out of the park on the old fortifications, into Boeveriestraat. Along here on the left is the newly renovated **De Moor Almshouse** (Godshuis

Walking in the park near the Old Water House

Map on pages 18–19

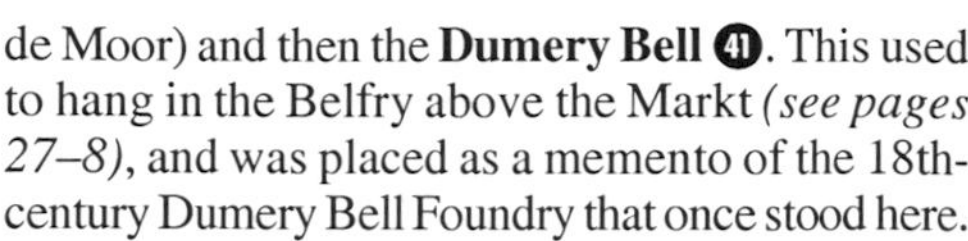

de Moor) and then the **Dumery Bell** 41. This used to hang in the Belfry above the Markt *(see pages 27–8)*, and was placed as a memento of the 18th-century Dumery Bell Foundry that once stood here.

On the right-hand side of the street lies the brick-built Benedictine cloister of **St Godelieve Abbey** (Sint-Godelieve Abdij) 42 (open Apr–Oct: daily 10am–noon and 2–6pm), whose nuns first moved into the city in the 16th century and established themselves in the abbey in 1623.

Below: the Dumery Bell
Bottom: 't Zand Square

'T ZAND SQUARE

A little further up the road, on the left, stands the **Capuchin Church** (Capucijnerkerk) 43. This is the church of the Capuchin Monastery, built here in 1869 to replace an earlier one that stood at what is now 't Zand. It was demolished to make way for the city's original railway station, which has itself vanished. At the top of the street and around the neighbouring streets are the almshouses **Van Campen** (1636), **Van Peenen** (1629), **Gloribus** (1634) and **Sucx** (1649).

And now we return to the wide and airy square called ★ **'t Zand** 44. In the city's early days, this area lay outside the original walls and was used for public gatherings and executions. One of the streets facing on to the square, **Vrijdagmarkt**, indicates that here was where the Friday Market

was once held, and the square's large size gives some idea of what an event this must have been. There's now a busy Saturday morning market here. **Dickie's Bar** at No. 16 does a nice line in tapas and Belgian beer.

As well as its graceful houses, cafés, shops and restaurants, 't Zand's most notable feature is the four strikingly large modern sculpture groups clustered around an ornamental fountain: **Bathing Women**, representing the cities of Bruges, Antwerp, Ghent and Kortrijk; **Landscape in Flanders**, being the polders; **The Fishermen**, recalling Bruges' links with the nearby North Sea coast; and **The Cyclists**, another image of the Flemish countryside, watched over by the local folk-tale characters Tijl Uilenspiegel *(see page 88)* and Nele. Travelling fairs regularly set up in 't Zand, which then becomes a noisy whirl of colour and light.

At the south end of the square is Bruges' world-class new **Concertgebouw** ㊺ concert and opera hall, a landmark of modern architecture built to accompany the city's 2002 tour of duty as a European Capital of Culture. The city tourist office and ticket sales office are based here.

For the love of beer

At 't Brugs Beertje café, across Steenstraat at 5 Kemelstraat, you can choose from 300 different beers, and even attend occasional lectures on the far from dry and dusty subject of Belgian beer.

GUILDHOUSES

If you want to return to the Markt and take in some shops on the way, you'll find them along Zuidzandstraat and Zilverstraat, with a diversion through the Zilverpand Shopping Gallery. This brings you, via Noordzandstraat and Sint-Amandstraat, back to the Markt.

Alternatively, you can go from Zuidzandstraat into **Steenstraat**. This is also a busy shopping street but has the added bonus of letting you see some former guildhouses on the way. There are four of these, headquarters of the trading and craft guilds which made such a big contribution to medieval life: these are the **Shoemakers' Guildhouse** at No. 40; the **Joiners' Guildhouse** at No. 38; the **Stonemasons' Guildhouse** at No. 25; and the **Bakers' Guildhouse** at No. 19. All are now shops or banks, but are an impressive sight with the tower of the Belfry rising above them.

Below: Tijl Uilenspiegel on 't Zand Square

5: Eastern Promise

St Peter's Chapel – St Walburga's Church – St Anne's Church – Jerusalem Church – Lace Centre – Municipal Folklore Museum – English Convent – St Sebastian's Archers' Guild – Guido Gezelle Museum – St George's Archers' Guild – Bruges Brewing and Malting Museum – De Gouden Boom Brewery

Below: Brugs Diamanthuis
Bottom: St Peter's Chapel

This route starts with a slew of historic and beautiful churches – although there may seem to be rather a lot of them, it's worth looking at them all to gain a real taste of Bruges' heritage. It then moves on eastwards out of the centre and into some of Bruges' most interesting and colourful museums, before ending up at a place where some liquid refreshment can pleasantly complement the educational experience.

ST PETER'S CHAPEL

Start at the Burg and leave via the little plane tree-dotted garden on its northern side, where St Donatian's Cathedral used to stand *(see pages 25–6)*, and Burgstraat. A little to the left, in Keersstraat, is **St Peter's Chapel** (Sint-Pieterskapel) ㊻, which for centuries was the chapel of the local Candlemakers' Guild until it was demolished in the 18th century. Rebuilt, it is now shared by the United Protestant and Anglican Churches.

Go around the church into Cordoeaniersstraat – which seems to have been named after the cordwainers (shoemakers) who toiled away here for the troops of the Count of Flanders, just as Wapenmakkersstraat at its end housed their armourers – pausing for a peek at the beautifully restored 1518 building with a stepped gable at No. 5. It is now a shop called the **Brugs Diamanthuis** and contains a sparkling display of diamonds.

ST WALBURGA'S CHURCH

Continue on through Sint-Jansplein, down Sint-Jansstraat as far as **Sint-Maartensplein** and ★★ **St Walburga's Church** (Sint-Walburgakerk) ㊼, a magnificent church dating from 1619–43, and designed by the Jesuit priest Pieter Huyssens. St Walburga's is one of the few baroque monuments in this determinedly Gothic city, with an elegant sufficiency of marble, and an altar, pulpit and communion bench that merit a visit.

Most of the interior decoration of the church was done by artists from Antwerp, among them Artus Quellin the Younger, Pieter Verbruggen and Jacob Cocx, a sign perhaps of how far Bruges had fallen in the artistic sphere.

Star Attraction
- **St Walburga's Church**

Jesuit founder

Ignatius de Loyola, the Spanish priest who founded the Jesuit Order in Paris in 1534 (it was formally approved by the Pope in 1540), was a frequent guest of the Spanish merchant Gonzalez d'Aguilera, between 1528 and 1530, in his house at No. 9 Spanjaardstraat. Loyola was also in regular contact in Bruges with the Spanish-born humanist philosopher Juan Luis Vivés.

THE JESUITS

The shock-troops of the Catholic Counter-Reformation, the Jesuits were very active in Bruges, which in the 16th century had flirted with Protestantism strongly enough for Calvinists to seize control of the city council for six years from 1578, and for monks and nuns to be chased away or executed. Spanish troops crushed the rebels in 1584 and the Jesuits moved in, taking up residence in Sint-Maartensplein, which they decked out over the years with a Jesuit monastery, a college and the church that is now St Walburga's. This alone survived the Jesuits' suppression in 1774, which has enabled it now to become the venue for concerts of church and classical music during the annual Festival of Flanders *(see page 102)*.

St Walburga's Church

SINT-ANNAREI

You may be getting just the teeniest bit weary by now of Bruges' seemingly endless parade of historical churches, but there are two more coming up in quick succession that are definitely worth a look. First take Hoornstraat and Verversdijk, where a plaque on the first canalside building to your right informs you that the local poet-priest Guido Gezelle lived here from 1867–72 *(see pages 63 and 101–2).*

Cross over the canal to **Sint-Annarei**, where you can make a short diversion left along the canal to see the restored baroque house at No. 22, and the merchant's house in Rococo style at No. 27. You can keep the diversion going a little longer by turning right at the end of Sint-Annarei into Blekersstraat, to the city's oldest tavern, the **Vlissinghe** at No. 2, dating from 1515, with Van Dyck period furniture and a pleasant garden terrace at the back.

Canal view
As a bonus, on the way to the Vlissinghe tavern, you get a fine view of the junction of two canals.

Below: Vlissinghe interior
Bottom: St-Annarei

ST ANNE'S CHURCH

Continue through Sint-Annakerkstraat to **Sint-Annaplein** and **★St Anne's Church** (Sint-Annakerk) ㊽. Not much to look at from the outside, St Anne's interior makes up for this with lavish baroque marble decoration that offsets the rather severe Gothic lines. Still, it's on a very

human scale and you get the impression it was done to make it comfortable for real people to worship in, rather than as some overstated monument to heavenly glory. It is certainly a popular place with the inhabitants of Bruges (insofar as any church is popular in the city, other than as a museum, in a city whose Catholicism seems to be honoured more in the breach than the observance, if attendance at Sunday Mass is anything to go by).

Star Attraction
- **Jerusalem Church**

Below and bottom: stained glass and crypt details in the Jerusalem Church

JERUSALEM CHURCH

From Sint-Annaplein, cross Jeruzalemstraat to Peperstraat and the striking ★★**Jerusalem Church** (Jeruzalemkerk; entrance with combined ticket for Lace Centre – *see page 60*) ㊾ at No. 3, built in the 15th century, mostly from 1471 to 1483 on a chapel dating from 1427, along the lines of the Church of the Holy Sepulchre in Jerusalem. This was done by scions of a wealthy merchant family of Genoese origin, long resident in Bruges and firmly allied to the House of Burgundy.

Pieter Adornes had made several pilgrimages to the Holy Land and brought back plans of the Church of the Holy Sepulchre that covers what is believed to be the Tomb of Christ. He set about recreating it in Bruges, and his son Anselm Adornes later financed its completion.

Anselm, a humanist and intellectual, was doing well in life until he made the fatal error of immersing himself in the treacherous morass of court intrigue in Scotland, when he was sent on a diplomatic mission to that country's King James III. He impressed the king but evidently not the king's opponents, who murdered him in 1483.

THE ADORNES FAMILY

Anselm's heart alone made the return trip to Bruges, to rest in a monumental tomb beside his wife Margaret's rather more complete remains in the Jerusalem Church. Their fine stone sarcophagus is surmounted by recumbent statues of the couple, and indeed the whole church is

Cottage lace
At its height, in 1840, lace-making in Bruges employed 10,000 women and girls out of a total population of 45,000. Although the Industrial Revolution was well underway by this time, this was still a cottage industry.

a monument to the Adornes family, with many other members also buried here.

Other notable sights within the church are the stained-glass windows from 1560 showing prominent members of the Adornes family, including Pieter and his wife Elisabeth, at prayer; a replica of the Tomb of Christ, complete with plaster statue, in the crypt underneath the choir; a tabernacle made from wrought iron; and the instruments of Christ's Passion on the altarpiece in the nave.

THE LACE CENTRE

From here we leave the churches behind for a while, and walk the few paces to the adjacent ★★★ **Lace Centre** (Kantcentrum) ㊿ (open Mon–Fri 10am–noon, 2–6pm; Sat 10am–noon, 2–5pm). This is housed in the former Jerusalem almshouses founded by the Adornes family in the 15th century.

The **lace workshop** is in what used to be the Adornes' mansion. In your travels around Bruges you may already have seen enough lace shops, and maybe even a surfeit of people making lace, to last two lifetimes. But the Lace Centre is appealing, being the place where the various strands come together.

The museum features notable antique exam-

Skilled hands at work, the Lace Centre

ples of lacework, while demonstrations of the painstaking art, which is undergoing a slow but steady revival, take place in the afternoon at the centre. In the museum shop you can buy all of the materials you need to have a go yourself.

Nearby in Balstraat is the **Lace School** (Kantschool), where the ancient art of lacemaking is passed on to the next generation, who will in turn fill up the city's shelves and window displays with handmade lace.

Star Attractions
- **The Lace Centre**
- **Municipal Folklore Museum**

Below: Folklore Museum from the outside
Bottom: one of the displays

BOBBIN LACE

Most lace made in Bruges is bobbin lace, a technique developed in Flanders in the 16th century, using pins around which threads of silk, linen or cotton are crossed and braided. It requires considerable delicacy, skill and concentration to manipulate up to 700 bobbins to achieve the kind of effect you can see in the gauzy dresses and lace ruffs in Renaissance portraits of wealthy individuals. Although most lace on sale in the city is machine-made, handmade lace in the distinctive *bloemenwerk* (flower lace), *rozenkant* (pearled rosary) and *toveressesteek* (fairy stitch) styles can still be found, and some shops deal only in the handmade product, which is of course much more expensive.

MUNICIPAL FOLKLORE MUSEUM

Keep going along Balstraat and on reaching the end turn left into Rolweg and the ★★**Museum of Folklore** (Museum voor Volkskunde) 51 (open Tues–Sun 9.30am–5pm). The museum is in the beautiful whitewashed cottages of the former Shoemakers' Guild almshouse.

It is an attractively simple place, with exhibition rooms using dummies to 'recreate' life in Bruges in times past: a primary school class led by a young priest, a cooper's workshop, spice shop, pipe room, milliner's workshop, confectioner's, household scenes and, maybe best of all, an old inn, **The Black Cat** (In De Zwarte Kat), which has genuine beer on tap. In summer, chil-

dren and adults both have a chance to play traditional games in the museum garden.

THE ENGLISH CONVENT

Cross Rolweg into Carmersstraat and make a right turn to pass the **English Convent** (Engels Klooster) ❺❷ at No. 85. As its name suggests, this was founded by an order of English nuns in 1629, and its domed church dates from 1736–9. The Flemish poet-priest Guido Gezelle *(see opposite)* died here, and his last words are carved on the facade: '…and I was so happy to hear the birds sing.' The English Convent was one of the focal points of the 'English Colony', which in the 1860s numbered 1,200 English people living in Bruges, most of them Catholics, though there was also an Anglican community centred on the Anglican Church in Ezelstraat (now the Joseph Ryelandt Hall; *see page 75*). If you want to see inside, wait at the entrance for one of the resident nuns to appear and guide you round. The highlight is the church itself, with its magnificent dome and lavish altar.

Below: the English Convent
Bottom: the convent's dome

ST SEBASTIAN'S ARCHERS' GUILD

Further up Carmersstraat, on the other side of the street, is the **St Sebastian's Archers' Guild**

(Schuttersgilde Sint-Sebastiaan) ⓹⓷ (open Tues–Thur 10am–noon and Sat 2–5pm). Far from being a bunch of weekend bow-and-arrow fanatics, the archers were a wealthy and influential force in the city, and their sumptuous 16th–17th-century quarters reflect this – their patron saint, a 3rd-century Christian martyr, had survived being shot with arrows only to be beaten to death.

Inside the guildhouse is a fine collection of arms and accoutrements, furnishings, gold and silver plate, paintings and other works of art. Among the guild's illustrious past members have been Belgian royalty, England's King Charles II, who in fact paid for the banqueting hall, and his brother Henry, who were both then in exile in Bruges from Oliver Cromwell. A portrait of Henry hangs above the fireplace.

Star Attraction
- **Guido Gezelle Museum**

Welcome break
At the end of Carmerstraat, the whitewashed Taverne De Verloren Hoek at No. 178 serves meals and drinks, and is a no doubt welcome place for a break.

GUIDO GEZELLE MUSEUM

Turn right into Kruisvest where you will see facing you the **St John's Windmill** *(see page 79)*, then go right again into Rolweg, where at No. 64 stands the ★★ **Guido Gezelle Museum** ⓹⓸ (open Tues–Sun 9.30am–12.30pm and 1.30–5pm). This museum is dedicated to the great Flemish poet and priest (1830–99) in the house that was his birthplace. Surrounded by a large garden, the rather gloomy brick-built house is interesting enough in its own right, and inside it contains objects relating to Gezelle's life and work, including copies of manuscripts and several editions of his writing.

Gezelle was something of a one-man Flemish literary industry, and had an important influence on both Dutch and Flemish modern literature. He catalogued around 150,000 words, phrases and proverbial sayings from the old Netherlandic dialect, published several journals and above all wrote poetry that recalled and aimed to help recreate the 'golden age' of Flemish rural and Roman Catholic society.

He was a founder-member of the Flemish Academy of Language and Literature and

Below: Taverne De Verloren Hoek, with St John's Windmill
Bottom: Guido Gezelle Museum plaque

received an honorary doctorate from the Catholic University of Leuven. Although Gezelle spent much of his career teaching and as a parish priest in Kortrijk, he returned to Bruges in his last year to be rector of the English Convent (for further information about Gezelle, *see pages 101–2*).

ST GEORGE'S ARCHERS' GUILD

Return to Kruisvest and pass the gardens known as the Guido Gezelle Warande, and the **Bonne Chière** wooden-stilt windmill *(see page 79)*, then turn right into Stijn Streuvelsstraat, where at No. 59 is **St George's Archers' Guild** (Schuttersgilde Sint-Joris) 55 (open on request only, tel: 050 448711). Unlike St Sebastian's boys, St George's were crossbowmen, and their ornate guildhouse contains a fine collection of crossbows, as well as the guild's archives. The garden, with a vertical target-mast and walkways protected from descending arrows, is like a park.

St George's Archers' Guild sign

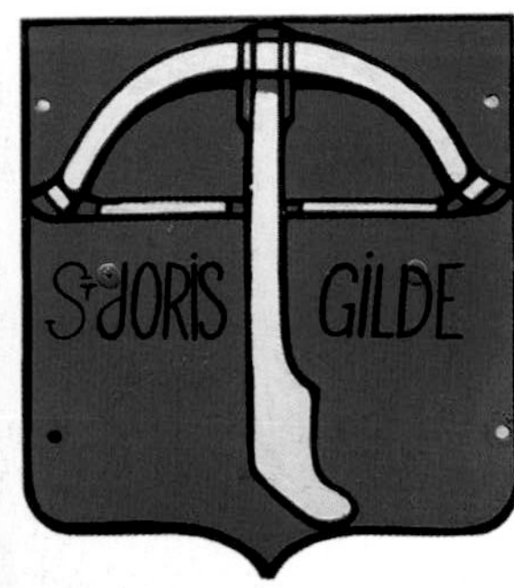

DE GOUDEN BOOM BREWERY

Continue along Stijn Streuvelsstraat (passing on the right the delightful **Godshuizen Paruitte** almshouses from 1897) to where it joins Peperstraat at the Jerusalem Church *(see page 59)*. Now go down Molenmeers and turn right on Langestraat. The Ter Reien Hotel at No. 1 occupies a 19th century canalside mansion where the artist Fernand Khnopff spent his childhood

The family moved to Brussels soon after the birth of his sister, Marguerite, who later served as a his model. Khnopff's melancholy fin-de-siècle paintings often included Bruges scenes, yet he rarely returned to his native city, preferring to rely instead on childhood memories and tourist postcards of Bruges.

One of the best views in Bruges is not far from here. Cross the road and stand on the cobbled terrace to look down the Groenrei canal, with the Belfry rising in the distance above the red tiled roofs. The cross the bridge and walk back to the Burg along Hoostraat.

6: Trading Places and Canalside Bruges

Map on pages 18–19

Royal Municipal Theatre – Genoese Lodge – Ter Beurze House – National House of Florence – Burghers' Lodge – Statue of Jan van Eyck – Toll House – De la Torre House – Easterners' House – Abbey of the Dunes – Our Lady of the Pottery – St Giles' Church – Augustinian Bridge – Sacred Heart Church

Star Attraction
- **Bruges Brewing and Malting Museum**

Although this route begins and ends in the old financial district north of the Markt, in many ways its highlight is the escape from the centre and its concerns, to the long and graceful canal that leads to the north edge of the old city.

Below: Gouden Handrei view
Bottom: Royal Municipal Theatre

ROYAL MUNICIPAL THEATRE

Starting in the Markt, leave by the north end of the square and take Vlamingstraat, crossing Kraanplein, named after a municipal crane that was used for loading and unloading barges on the canal at this point – but both crane and canal have vanished. On the left side of the road, at No. 29, is the **Royal Municipal Theatre** (Koninklijke Stadsschouwburg) ❺❽. This neoclassical building, which has a colonnaded upper facade dating from 1869, was Bruges' main venue for opera, classical music, theatre and dance until

the Concertgebouw opened in 2002. In front of it is a sculpture representing Papageno from Mozart's *The Magic Flute*.

A few doors along, at No. 33, is the ★ **Genoese Lodge** (Genuese Loge) 59, dating from 1399, which was the headquarters of the merchants of Genoa, based in the city until they packed up and left around 1520. It was then used as a cloth exchange, the Saaihalle, for a few centuries, and is now a cultural centre. The bell-gable was added in 1720.

Burgher's Lodge bear – a badge of the city

Ter Beurze House

On the opposite corner, across Grauwwerkersstraat, at No. 35, is ★ **Ter Beurze House** (Huis Ter Beurze) 60, which has a plaque with the year 1453 on the facade and an interesting story attached to it. It used to be an inn and money-changing operation run by the Van den Beurze family, and was frequented by so many foreign merchants and bankers that the surroundings became known as the Beursplein. It is from this that the word 'Bourse', the common international name for a stock exchange, comes. Given its history, the Ter Beurze House should feel perfectly comfortable in its current role – as a branch of the KBC Bank.

A short way into Grauwwerkersstraat, at Nos. 2–4, is a house with an original 13th-century facade. From here cross Vlamingstraat to Academiestraat and the **National House of Florence** 61. Dating from 1430 but much refurbished over the centuries, this is where Florentine merchants once had their base in the city. The facade, which is unusual in that it has a slight concave curve, has a plaque quoting a passage from Dante's *The Divine Comedy* referring to Bruges, and the building now houses the ultra-smart restaurant De Florentijnen.

Burghers' Lodge

A little further along Academiestraat, at Nos. 14–18, is the late-Gothic ★ **Burghers' Lodge** (Poortersloge) 62, another of the important buildings in this part of town where prominent merchants and bankers used to meet. The ornate 15th-century lodge, with a high bell-tower, was until 1890 the City Academy. Restored in the early 1900s, it now houses the Bruges National Archive. When it was first built it was also the headquarters of an exclusive local society called De Witte Beer (The White Bear), which among other activities organised jousting tournaments. Look for the statue, dating from 1417, of a bear carrying a shield with masonic symbols, a badge of the city, standing in a niche at the end of the facade, recalling this part of its history.

Star Attraction
• Jan van Eyckplein

Nice work
Jan van Eyck sued by proxy for Isabella of Portugal's hand on behalf of Philip the Good of Burgundy. As part of this virtual-wooing process he was required to lie with one leg bare on a bed beside the intended bride. He must have made a pretty good job of this, as Philip and Isabella tied the knot in 1430.

JAN VAN EYCK SQUARE

Another, and no doubt more important, statue can be seen on neighbouring ★★ **Jan van Eyckplein.** It is a **statue of Jan van Eyck** 63, the Flemish artist *(see page 97)* who lived and worked in Bruges from 1425 until his death in 1441. He stands with his back to the canal at Spiegelrei. Across the road at No. 2 is the ★ **Toll House** (Tolhuis) 64. Built in 1477–8, it was where taxes were levied on goods brought into the city by boat. It reopened in 2000 after refurbishment to house West Flanders Province's archives and an information centre. Note the heraldic device above the

Below: Toll House portal detail
Bottom: Jan van Eyckplein

entrance inscribed with insignia of the Order of the Golden Fleece, founded in Bruges in 1430 *(see page 51)*.

Adjacent to this, Spanjaardstraat was the centre of the Spanish mercantile community in the 16th century and the many mansions in this area testify to their wealth. Among the best of these, at No. 16, is the ★**De la Torre House** (65), which has an ornately decorated Renaissance portal. The house now belongs to a clinic. Ignatius de Loyola, the Spanish priest who founded the Jesuits, was a frequent guest in the house at No. 9 between 1528 and 1530.

Trading Places
During the Middle Ages, Bruges was a key member of the powerful Baltic-based Hanseatic League trading alliance, hosting the most important of the league's four principal *kontore* (foreign outposts).

EASTERNERS' HOUSE

Return to Jan van Eyckplein – perhaps pausing for a look at the stone frontage dating from around 1300 at No. 6 – and turn into Woensdagmarkt, where there is a statue of the German-born painter and resident of Bruges Hans Memling *(see pages 98–100)*. In the adjacent Genthof, at No. 7, is one of Bruges' two surviving houses with wooden facades, built in the 15th century (its lower section has, however, now been replaced with brick).

Connected to Woensdagmarkt and Oosterlingenplein is Krom Genthof, where at No. 1 stands the ★**Easterners' House** (Oosterlingenhuis) (66), once the local headquarters of the Hanseatic League, which was trading with Bruges as early as the 13th century. It was built from 1478 to 1481, but only part of it survives in what is now the Hotel Bryghia *(see page 117)*.

Hans Memling statue

POTTERIEREI

Now comes a long walk into an area worlds apart from the busy city centre, over the canal bridge (reached either via Genthof or from the Easterners' House along attractive **Gouden Handrei**), into **Potterierei**. This relaxing canalside stroll offers a glimpse of 'ordinary' Bruges, and it is indicative of this city's great beauty that it lacks little, or nothing, of the splendour of better-advertised locations. Simply enjoy the houses, the canal views and bridges, and the peace and quiet. If you enjoy Japanese food and have a healthy budget, **Koto** in the De' Medici Hotel at No. 15 is a good place to stop for a meal *(see page 106)*.

Near the far end of Potterierei, at No. 72, you can pass through a wooden gateway into the **Abbey of the Dunes** (Duinenabdij) 67. This foundation was once based by the sea at Koksijde on the North Sea coast – hence its name – but it was forced to retreat from encroaching waters in 1560, and in the 17th century set up shop here in Bruges. Since 1833 it has been the Episcopal Seminary. You can visit its 18th-century church, gardens and greenhouse with permission, obtainable (perhaps) at the main entrance.

Star Attraction
• Our Lady of the Pottery

OUR LADY OF THE POTTERY

Continue up Potterierei to Nos. 78–79, which is the location of ★★ **Our Lady of the Pottery** (Onze-Lieve-Vrouw van de Potterie) 68, whose recorded history goes back to 1276. Like St John's Hospital *(see page 44)*, it began life as a hospice and developed as such from the 14th to the 17th centuries. Most of the complex is now a senior citizens' home, but part of it – including a ward and the 14th–15th-century cloisters – has been

Below and bottom: aspects of Potterierei

opened as the ★★**Potterie Museum** (open Tues–Sun 9.30am–12.30pm and 1.30–5pm). In here is displayed a rich collection of tapestries, 15th–17th-century furniture in styles ranging from Gothic to baroque, silverware, religious objects and books, as well as some early Flemish paintings.

The adjoining 14th-century ★**church**, which used to be the chapel of the Potters' Guild, is a little gem, with a superb baroque interior containing, among other treasures, a 13th-century statue of Our Lady of the Pottery that is said to have miraculous powers, and a 16th-century tapestry of the Nativity.

Below: drawbridge and Langerei
Bottom: St Giles' Church

A Bridge to Cross

If you continue northwards and around the corner, you'll reach the canal basin at Dampoort with the excellent Du Phare Bistro *(see page 80)*. However, this makes for quite a hike if you want to return to the centre. Instead, walking back along Potterierei, at the first bridge (a drawbridge), cross over to **Langerei**, and continue south past the restored **Sareptha** at Nos. 25–26. This was formerly the Convent of the Augustinian Canonesses, who moved here in 1617 and stayed until they were turfed out by Emperor Joseph II in 1784. It is now an educational institution.

St Giles' Church

Shortly after, turn right into Sint-Gilliskoorstraat, which leads to ★**St Giles' Church** (Sint-Gilliskerk) ❻❾. This parish church was founded around 1241 and built in the early Gothic style, but was drastically altered in the 15th century, leaving it with three aisles in place of the earlier cruciform shape. Among the treasures to be seen inside are a superb organ, and a cycle of paintings from 1774 by Bruges artist Jan Garemijn depicting the history of the Trinitarian Brothers.

The painter Hans Memling *(see pages 98–100)* was buried here in 1494 in the no longer extant churchyard.

AUGUSTINIAN BRIDGE

Come out into Sint-Gilliskerkstraat, right into Gouden-Handstraat, and return to the waterside at Spaanse Loskaai beside the 13th-century **Augustinian Bridge** (Augustijnenbrug) ⓻⓪, with its old stone benches that were once used by street traders for displaying their wares. Then cross over and either stroll to the left along handsome canal-side Spaanse Loskaai and Gouden Handrei, or turn right into Korte Winkel, which leads into Vlamingstraat. At No. 100, look for the house built for goldsmith Herman van Houtvelde in 1514 – you get a fine view of its rear facade from the adjacent bridge, Vlamingbrug.

Around the corner in Korte Winkel, is one of only two surviving wooden facades in Bruges, also dating from the early 16th century.

Below: the facade at 100 Vlamingstraat
Bottom: Augustinian Bridge

SACRED HEART CHURCH

Also in Vlamingstraat is the **Sacred Heart Church** (Heilige Hartkerk) ⓻① at No. 84. This neo-Gothic church dating from 1879–85 used to belong to the Jesuit Order and has now been renovated as a theatre, called Celebrations Entertainment, and is the venue for the popular **Brugge Anno 1468** (Bruges Year 1468) medieval banquet and theatrical show, with actors playing aristocrats, jesters and minstrels *(see page 107)*.

7: West to the Donkey Gate

De Biekorf City Library and Civic Hall – Municipal Conservatory – Butter House – Gistel House – Bladelin House – Original City Walls – Carmelite Church – Joseph Rylandt Hall – Donkey Gate – St James's Church

This fairly short route begins at the Markt and takes in several of Bruges' historic patrician houses. It passes through the site of the city's original defensive walls, before visiting one of the surviving gates in the later walls. The finale is St James's Church, whose interior benefited greatly from the patronage of the city's aristocrats.

Below: Sint-Jakobsstraat with St James's Church
Bottom: Eiermarkt

LIBRARY AND CIVIC HALL

Leave the Markt by the northwest corner, leading past Eiermarkt with its Rococo water pump from 1761 by the sculptor Pieter Peper, into Kuipersstraat, where a short way along, at No. 3, is **De Biekorf City Library and Civic Hall** ⓬. If you continue down this street you will see the fine 15th-century Black House (Zwart Huis) at No. 23, now a tavern.

Returning to Eiermarkt, turn right into Sint-Jakobsstraat. On the left at No. 13 is the turn-of-the-century Art Nouveau facade of a rather good and moderately priced bistro, **Pietje Pek** *(see*

page 107). A little further along, at Nos. 23–25, is the **Municipal Conservatory** (Stedelijk Conservatorium) ⓻⓷, housed in an impressive neoclassical townhouse dating from the 18th century, the Hotel van Borssele. Walk in – pretend you're a student or a maestro – and swing right through a waiting-room to admire the restored stone facades around an inner courtyard; across the road at Nos. 20–26 is a Cultural Centre.

Star Attraction
- **Bladelin House**

BUTTER HOUSE

Continuing along Sint-Jakobsstraat, on the right you reach the **Butter House** (Boterhuis) 74 at No. 38, a turreted and arched 16th-century complex where dairy products were sold from the 17th century. It now houses the **De Lumière art cinema**, a hotel and an antiques shop.

Pass under the archway into Naaldenstraat, where No. 7 is the **Gistel House** (Hof van Gistel) 75, a city mansion built by the Duke of Vendôme, Antoine de Bourbon. Further along, at No. 19, you come to an even more impressive mansion, the 15th-century ★★ **Bladelin House** (Hof Bladelin) 76. The inner courtyard can be visited (open Apr–Sept: Mon–Sat 10am–noon and 2–5pm, Sun 10.30am–noon; Oct–Mar: Mon–Sat 10am–noon and 2–4pm, Sun 10.30am–noon). But the interior, a senior citizens' home, can be seen only by appointment (tel: 050 336434); ring the doorbell and see if one of the nuns has time to take you on an exhaustive guided tour.

Below: cinema entrance adjacent to the Black House
Bottom: neo-Gothic niche on Bladelin House

HISTORY OF BLADELIN HOUSE

The mansion was built by Pieter Bladelin (1410–72), who was treasurer to Philip the Good, Duke of Burgundy. Note the neo-Gothic niche (1892) on the outer facade showing Bladelin kneeling before a crowned Madonna and Child. This job was obviously a nice little earner, enabling him to build the handsome mansion, dabble in polder reclamation, found the village of Middelburg 20km (12 miles) east of Bruges

Lunch stop
For a break, you can try one of 60 different kinds of pancake at the rustic Crêperie de Bretoen in Ezelstraat at No. 4.

beside the Dutch border, and become a patron of Flemish artists, including Rogier van der Weyden (1399–1464).

The Medici Bank of Florence took over the house in 1466, and it is this connection that has given it an Italianate look, including the Renaissance courtyard and ornamental garden, which is thought to be the earliest example of the Renaissance style in the Low Countries. On the courtyard facade are two medallions dating from 1469, depicting Lorenzo de' Medici (Lorenzo the Magnificent) and his wife Clarisse Orsini.

Below: Pottenmakkersstraat

THE CITY WALLS

Continue to Grauwwerkersstraat and turn left. As you walk towards the canal bridge you are following the line of the original **city walls** ⓱. These were built in the 12th century , thrown up around the inner canal circuit in the aftermath of Charles the Good's assassination. Their purpose was to defend what was then a much smaller city than that enclosed by the second line of circumvallation, whose outline is preserved today by the ring canal and a park dating from the 14th century.

A fine surviving stretch of this old inner wall stands along the canal at this point, including part of a defensive tower dating from 1127, which can be seen in the back garden of one of the houses to your right (although you will get a better view of it from Pottenmakkersstraat on the other side of the water).

THE CARMELITES

Cross over the canal by the **Donkey Bridge** (Ezelbrug) into Ezelstraat, where the Handelskamer (Chamber of Commerce) is on the left at No. 25. At No. 2 stands the 15th-century **Carmelite Church** (Karmelietenkerk) ⓲, with a gloomy baroque interior dating from 1688–91, belonging to the big **Carmelite Monastery** that has occupied the former Hof van Uitkerke here since 1633. The monastery is a very unusual looking building, perhaps because it was built by monks who also had the care of plague victims on their minds at the time. The Carmelites were shown the door by the French in 1795 but returned in the 19th century, and the church is one of the few places in Bruges occupied by religious men and women where you are actually likely to see any of them.

JOSEPH RYLANDT HALL

Continue along Ezelstraat to the **Joseph Rylandt Hall** (Joseph Rylandtzaal) ⑲ at Achiel Van Ackerplein. This was once the convent church of the Carmelites, but was taken over by Bruges' large English community in the 1820s to serve as their Anglican church. Since 1983 it has been a concert hall belonging to the city, taking its name from the Bruges composer Joseph Rylandt (1870–1965); recitals and other performances are held here. The sculpture group on the facade represents the *Art of Music,* and in front of the hall is a self-satisfied looking statue of the Bruges politician Achiel van Acker (1898–1975), who was Belgian Minister of State.

A short way further up the street on the left, at No. 115, is the **Orthodox Church of Saints Constantine and Helena**, and beyond that the dense undergrowth of the **Pastor van Haecke Garden** (Pastoor van Haecke Plantsoen).

Below: carving on the Carmelite Church
Bottom: Joseph Rylandt Hall

THE DONKEY GATE

At the end of Ezelstraat, cross over Koningin Elisabethlaan to the restored ★★ **Donkey Gate** (Ezelpoort), or **St James's Gate** (Sint-Jacobspoort) ⑧⓪, one of four surviving gates in the city wall out of the original nine. It was built in 1369–70 on the road out to Ostend, and has been rebuilt several times. A more appropriate name for this formidable looking bastion today would be the 'Swan's Gate', after the number of swans that cruise the canal beside it.

Below: Donkey Gate
Bottom: Holy Family

From here go left for a short distance on **Gulden-Vlieslaan**, then take another left into Gieterijstraat and then right into Rozendal. This takes you past the **Sint-Joos Almshouse** at the southern end of Pastor van Haecke Garden, the Holy Family Technical Institute (Technische Instituut van de Heilige Familie),which was once a convent, and the **Maricolen Convent**. It's not exactly an exciting diversion, but it saves you from simply retracing your footsteps.

If you turn left into Oude Zak, this brings you back by way of the Ezelbrug (Donkey Bridge), across the canal into Sint-Jakobsstraat.

ST JAMES'S CHURCH

Turn right to Sint-Jakobsplein, and you will find ★★ **St James's Church** (Sint-Jakobskerk) ⑧①. This is a heavy-looking Gothic construction built in the 1240s over an earlier chapel, and rebuilt in the 15th century with a thick-set tower. But its true beauty lies within.

The church benefited from its position close to the Prinsenhof *(see pages 50–51)*, an area that attracted the rich and influential who wanted to own houses where they could more easily see and be seen by the monarch. Much of the interior decoration and paintings were paid for by those wealthy Burgundian worthies. Look in particular at the intricately carved wooden pulpit, with figures at its base representing the continents. In the nave is the triptych of *The Legend of St Lucy*, dating from 1480 *(see box)*, by an artist known simply as the Master of the Legend of St Lucy.

Legend of St Lucy
The tryptych of The Legend of St Lucy in St James' Church depicts the saint, martyred around 304 in Sicily during the persecution of Diocletian, giving away her worldly goods to the poor and being sentenced to a life of prostitution, to which not even two oxen are strong enough to drag her.

8: Along the Ring Canal Park

Powder Tower – Gentpoort City Gate – Queen Astrid Park – Blessed Mary Magdalene Church – Holy Cross Gate – Bonne Chière Windmill – St John's Windmill – Nieuwe Papegaai Windmill – Koeleweimolen – Dampoort – Noorweegse Kaai jetty

Star Attractions
- **Donkey Gate**
- **St James's Church**

This route follows the line of the ring canal and a narrow park that runs around the southern and eastern stretches of what used to be the city walls – long since demolished – which encompassed a circuit of 6.8km (4¼ miles), and is punctuated by two of the remaining four fortified gates of those walls. It can be done either on foot or by bicycle *(see page 112)*; a bike would give you more freedom, and allow you to cover the western stretch of the canal as well, whose points of interest are covered in other itineraries *(see page 49 and page 72)*.

Below: Blessed Mary Magdalene Church
Bottom: ring canal view

The Powder Tower

Start on Begijnenvest, at the southern end of the Lake of Love *(see page 46)*, beside the ★ **Powder Tower** (Poertoren) ❽❷. Dating from 1398, this is the only one of the city walls' defensive towers to have survived, and is named after the gunpowder that used to be stored within it. Behind

In memoriam
Koningin Astridpark is named after the popular Queen Astrid, wife of King Leopold III. She was killed in 1935 in a road accident in Switzerland while the king was driving their car.

Below: Tailor's Guild Almshouse emblem
Bottom: Queen Astrid Park

you is the start of the **Ghent Canal** (Gentse Vaart), which naturally leads to Ghent. Go eastwards out of the Minnewater Park, past the former Convent of the Poor Clares to your left, the Katelijnepoort Bridge over the canal to your right, the **Tailors' Guild Almshouse** on your left, and keep going north through the park as it curves around anticlockwise following the line of the ring canal round on your right.

QUEEN ASTRID PARK

You come next to the ⋆ **Gentpoort City Gate** ❽❸, a great lump of medieval brickwork that was put together in two phases, part dating from 1361–3 and part from 1401–6. Today, although it still looks powerful and impressive, it's little more than a glorified traffic-calming measure at the exit from the old city.

Turn left here on Gentpoortstraat to the ⋆ **Queen Astrid Park** (Koningin Astridpark) ❽❹, one of several parks bequeathed to the city by the demise of the monastery or convent that once stood there – in this case a Franciscan Abbey, demolished in 1578 during the brief Protestant ascendancy in the city. You rarely find tourists here and can admire in peace the blue-and-gold-painted, wrought-iron bandstand, dating from 1859, and watch the swans swimming around the central pond.

NEO-GOTHIC CHURCH

In compensation for the loss of the abbey, there is, however, the **Blessed Mary Magdalene Church** (Heilige-Magdelenekerk) ❽❺ on the corner of Staalijzerstraat and Schaarstraat. A neo-Gothic edifice, it was built in 1851–3. The park itself is one of Bruges' biggest, and a tranquil oasis. It is bordered by two almshouses, the **De Fontaine Almshouse** and the **Bakers' Guild Almshouse**.

Follow Schaarstraat to the **Coupure Bridge** over the canal, from where you can watch fishermen waiting for a bite and see yachts and cabin cruisers moored to the quay. Turn right after the bridge to the **Marieke sculpture**, portraying the girl – and the wistful memory of first love – in the great Belgian singer Jacques Brel's song *Ai Marieke* (1961). The adjacent **Bistro De Schaar** at No. 2 Hooistraat is a good place for a break.

Returning to the ring canal park at Kazernevest and following it round, you reach ★ **Holy Cross Gate** (Kruispoort) ❽❻, a castle-like fortified gate with a drawbridge, built between 1366 and 1368 and substantially rebuilt from 1401 to 1406.

Star Attraction
- **St John's Windmill**

Below: Marieke sculpture
Bottom: barge near St John's Windmill

Windmills in the Park

The pathway through the park now runs parallel to Kruisvest, and leads in quick succession to no fewer than four windmills, recalling the many mills that once stood along the city walls. The first you encounter is the ★ **Bonne Chière Windmill** ❽❼, which stands on wooden stilt supports. This is no native of Bruges, but a long-term resident, having been built in 1888 at Olsene in East Flanders and moved to its present location in 1911. It is no longer in use, however.

In contrast, ★★ **St John's Windmill** (Sint-Janshuismolen) ❽❽ is very much in operation throughout the summer as a museum piece, with a miller to show visitors around (open May–Sept: Tues–Sun 9.30am–12.30pm, 1.30–5pm). This

venerable structure earned a living by twirling its blades in the wind here from 1770 to 1914, and was restored in 1964.

Continuing north, you come next to the ★ **Nieuwe Papegaai Windmill** 89, which was used as an oil-mill at Beveren-IJzer in West Flanders and rebuilt here in 1970. It is no longer in use.

The final mill of the quartet is the ★ **Koeleweimolen** 90 (open June–Sept: 9.30am–12.30pm, 1.30–5pm), dating from 1765 and employed at Meulebeke in West Flanders until it was rebuilt here in 1996.

Below: docking at Dampoort
Bottom: Du Phare Bistro

The Dampoort

Continuing to the end of the park brings you to the **Dampoort** 91 and the adjacent Handelskom Docks excavated in 1664–65 to take advantage of the new network of inland waterways passing through Bruges, and once used by sea-going vessels.

This is a part of the Old Dock and is often still busy with canal barges, as it is close to the start of the Baudouin Canal (Boudewijnkanaal) to Zeebrugge and the canal to Ostend which, from 1622 onwards, restored the city's lost link with the sea. It is also where the road leaves the city for the attractive nearby Flemish village of **Damme**, which is well renowned for its restaurants *(see pages 86–90)*.

Beside the dock, along Komvest, are the Art Deco offices of the former (now demolished) Brugse Gistfabriek, dating from 1925. It now houses the Dutch consulate in Bruges.

If you're feeling hungry or thirsty, the **Du Phare Bistro** adjacent to the canal basin is a good bet. The food is excellent, and if you're here in the evening there may be some live jazz going on.

Noorweegse Kaai

This puts you close to the **jetty** 92 on **Noorweegse Kaai**, from where a stern-wheel paddle steamer, the *Lamme Goedzaak*, makes excursions along the Bruges–Sluis Canal to Damme *(see page 87)*.

Environs of Bruges

Even if you're only in Bruges for a short stay, it's well worth venturing out to see what lies beyond the city centre. Attractions in the vicinity include theme parks, castles, abbeys and an assortment of pleasant villages, all of them popular destinations for the people of Bruges and many of them have plenty of things to interest children. *(See map on page 83.)*

Olympiapark

If walking all over Bruges hasn't been enough exercise for you, maybe what you need is a visit to this multipurpose sports centre in Sint-Andries, west of the city centre. There's an Olympic-size swimming pool, a roller-skating rink, and facilities for tennis, squash and other participant sports. In addition, Bruges' two soccer outfits, Club Brugge KV and Cercle Brugge KSV, both play at the complex's Jan Breydel Stadium.

BEISBROEK AND TUDOR CITY PARKS

These two big country estates stand side by side in the forests just a short distance southwest of Bruges, off Koning Albert I-Laan.★ **Beisbroek**, covering 80 hectares (200 acres), has trees, heathland, footpaths, picnic areas, a deer compound, a cafeteria, a castle that serves as an interactive **Nature Centre** (open Apr–Nov: Mon–Fri 2–5pm, Sun 2–6pm; Mar: Sun 2–6pm), a **Planetarium** (shows Wed and Sun at 3 and 4.30pm, Fri at 8.30pm; during school holidays, also Mon, Tues, Thur at 3pm) and an **Observatory** (open Fri 8pm).

At the **Tudor City Park**, which covers 40 hectares (100 acres), there is a botanical garden, and beehives and the splendid **Tudor Castle**, which is now a classy restaurant and seminar and reception centre.

Below: Beisbroek observatory
Bottom: rhododendrons in the forest

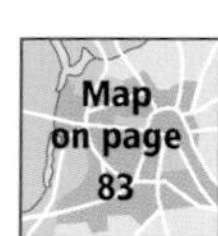

Below: Boudewijn park
Bottom: St Trudo Abbey stained glass

BOUDEWIJN THEME PARK

The ⋆**Boudewijn Seapark** has a dolphinarium, and is located in the southern suburbs of Bruges at No. 12 De Baeckestraat (open Easter holidays: daily 10am–5pm; May–June Thur–Tues 10am–5pm; July–Aug: daily 10am–6pm; first three weeks Sept: Tues, Sat and Sun 10am–5pm). It is naturally a big favourite with children, and could easily form part of a family 'deal', whereby the adults explore Bruges' historic treasures on condition that the kids get to play on the rides and boats, and see the dolphins and orca ('killer' whale) here. There are also two traditional old barrel organs, and a giant astronomical clock called the Heirmanklok on show. In fact, the adults may find they enjoy the park just as much as the children.

CASTLE OF THE COUNTS

The short trip out to **Male** on the eastern fringe of Bruges is worthwhile for anyone interested in the history of the city, because what is now the ⋆**St Trudo Abbey** (Sint-Trudo Abdij) of the Sisters of the Holy Sepulchre was at one time the Castle of the Counts of Flanders.

Much has changed since the castle was built in the 12th century by Count Philip of Alsace (Filip van de Elzas) – in fact everything has changed, as the original castle was destroyed by rebels from Ghent in 1382, and has been rebuilt and destroyed again by military action or by accidental fire regularly throughout the centuries.

Still, the vast moated castle-turned-abbey, in which you can visit the Hall of the Knights (Ridderzaal) in the restored 14th-century keep and the church, gives a good indication of the power and wealth of the former rulers of Flanders.

DUDZELE

This small village beside the Boudewijn Canal north of Bruges is not really worth visiting for itself alone. However, if you are cycling or driving to Lissewege *(see opposite)*, it lies on the most scenic route and it makes sense to look at the ruined 12th-century Romanesque tower at the **Church of St Peter in Chains** (Sint-Pieters-Banden) in the centre. Across the road is the small **De Groene Tente Museum of Regional History** (reopened August 2006).

At the **Gallo-Roman Wine-House**, 1 Westkapelsesteenweg, you can watch mead (honey wine) being produced and you can also experience a Roman costume banquet here, if you arrange it in advance (tel: 050 599599).

Fort Beieren

Between the village of Koolkerke and the Damme Canal, 4km (2½ miles) northeast of Bruges, this earthworks fort, dating from 1704, and the vestiges of a demolished castle, are set in what is now a small country park of 26 hectares (65 acres). It makes a pleasant target for a country stroll, or more likely a brief diversion if you are doing the excursion to Damme *(see page 86)*.

LISSEWEGE

This engagingly pretty village north of Bruges, on the road to Zeebrugge, makes a great destination for a cycling excursion or a short drive from the city. The whitewashed old houses are a handsome sight in themselves, and form what

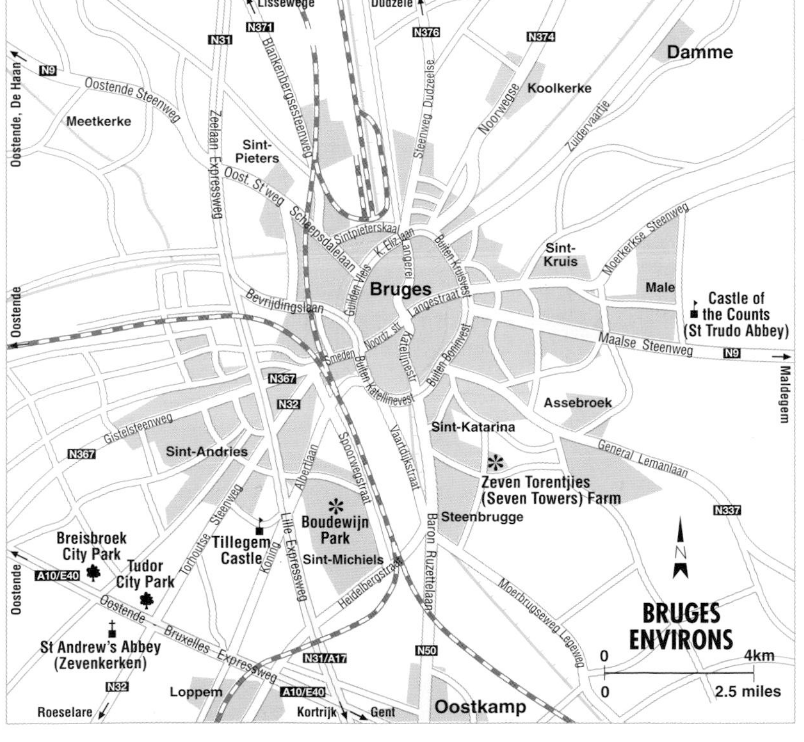

is reckoned to be the best-preserved rural community on the Flemish coastal plain. Look out for the **Lissewege Waterway** (Lisseweegs Vaartje), a narrow canal passing through the village that in medieval times connected it with Bruges.

In the main square, Onder de Toren, stands the huge early Gothic **Church of Our Lady** (Onze-Lieve-Vrouwekerk), dating from 1225–50, with a flat-topped tower 50m (164ft) high, from which a carillon tune bursts forth occasionally. Inside, you'll find a superb baroque organ, some interesting 17th- and 18th-century paintings, and a replica of the miraculous statue of the Madonna and Child destroyed by Dutch Protestants in the 16th century.

Blaze of colour
From April until the end of September, the banks of the Lissewege Waterway inside the village are decked with thousands of flowers and flowering plants. You can take in this blaze of floral colour on a pleasant stroll along the canalside Valerius de Saedeleer path.

The ★**Historical Museum** at No. 6 Walram Romboudtstraat displays a collection of archaeological finds from the area. Some of those artefacts concern the former **Ter Doest Abbey**, which you pass on the way from Bruges, and which was destroyed by Dutch rebels in the 16th century. All that remains of it is a remarkable Gothic barn dating from 1250, which is still used by the manor farm that replaced the abbey in the 1650s. The farm also houses a fine country restaurant, the **Hof ter Doest** *(see page 106)*.

Church of Our Lady

St Andrew's Abbey

If you haven't had enough of the abbey habit in Bruges itself, then **St Andrew's** (Sint-Andries), a big Benedictine abbey at **Zevenkerken**, makes a good side trip. To the southwest of Bruges on Torhoutse Steenweg, it was founded around 1100 and rebuilt in the 19th century after being destroyed by the Revolutionary French at the end of the 18th. The abbey is situated amid forests, and its monks produce fine pottery as well as icons. There is a popular cafeteria, the **Benediktusheem**, that serves cheap and cheerful food.

Tillegembos Provincial Estate

West Flanders Province's tourist office has set itself up in the ★★**Tillegem Castle** (Kasteel Tillegem) at the heart of this splendid country estate, covering 105 hectares (260 acres) south-west of Bruges, so if you want to see more of this part of Belgium you've come to the right place for information.

The 14th-century castle is surrounded by a moat, in which a pair of black swans glide, and a forested area that is pleasant for a walk.

Star Attraction
- **Tillegem Castle**

SEVEN TOWERS FARM

A 14th-century former feudal manor farm and estate, ★ **Seven Towers Farm** (Zeven Torentjes) on Canadaring, Assebroek, in Bruges' eastern suburbs, has been turned into a children's farm, complete with pigs, hens, horses, rabbits and many other animals. There is also a blacksmith, who performs demonstrations of the old skill, and free horse-and-carriage rides. The cafeteria serves drinks and meals.

CASTLE LOPPEM

A Flemish neo-Gothic castle, completed in 1863, **Castle Loppem** (Kasteel Loppem), south of Bruges, was the residence of Belgium's 'Soldier King' Albert I and his family during the fading months of World War I. It houses art and antiques from the 16th and 17th centuries, and religious sculptures from the 13th to the 16th centuries.

Below: Tillegem Castle
Bottom: Seven Towers Farm

Excursion to Damme

Although Bruges has enough sights to keep anyone on a short break fully occupied, if you have more time you could visit Damme, just 8km (5 miles) away. The village is famed for its beauty, attractive location beside the canal from Bruges to Sluis, and 15th-century Town Hall. Damme is every bit as handsome as Bruges, but a lot smaller and easier to get to grips with, and has a main street lined with fine, typically Flemish restaurants. Most visitors go to Damme to get to grips with the knives and forks in those restaurants, but strolling around also has its devotees.

Below: just one of Damme's many bookshops
Bottom: the Town Hall

FLEMISH VILLAGE OF BOOKS

Damme has reinvented itself in recent years as the Flemish Village of Books, modelled on England's Hay-on-Wye and Redu in the Belgian Ardennes. A dozen bookshops sell second-hand and rare editions and have attracted a cultured clientele.

From the 12th century to the 16th, Damme played a major role as the outer harbour of Bruges, where sea-going vessels loaded and unloaded their cargo. But by 1520, the Zwin inlet had silted up, blocking off access to the sea and ending the prosperity of both Bruges and Damme. The Duke of Burgundy, Charles the Bold, and Margaret of

York, the sister of England's King Edward IV, held their wedding here in the village in 1468, an indication of its importance at that time.

Star Attraction
- **Paddle Steamer**

PADDLE STEAMER

A small stern-wheel ★★ **paddle steamer**, the *Lamme Goedzak,* leaves from the jetty at Noorweegse Kaai in the north of Bruges, just beyond Dampoort, for a half-hour cruise to Damme (the No. 4 bus – *see page 111* – connects Dampoort with Bruges city centre and railway station). From April to September the paddle steamer sails five times a day along the poplar-lined canal, and past the Schellemolen windmill, to tie up beside Damme's main street.

One way of spending a pleasant day, especially if the weather is good, is to sail to Damme, have lunch at one of the restaurants, then stroll around for a while before returning by boat. In addition, the Sightseeing Line's minibuses are frequent visitors to Damme, leaving from the Markt in Bruges (with the option of returning on the *Lamme Goedzak*). You can also drive, cycle or even walk there. More information is available from Damme Tourist Office, tel: 050 288610.

The Lamme Goedzak and Schellemolen

DAMME TOWN HALL

The Gothic ★ **Town Hall** (Stadhuis) ❶ in the Markt dates from 1464–8, and was paid for with taxes on the wine and herring that used to pass through the port to be traded in other countries. On its facade are statues of, among others, Charles the Bold, Margaret of York, Count Philip of Alsace and Countess Johanna and Countess Margaret of Constantinople.

In front of the Town Hall stands a statue of the scholar-poet Jacob van Maerlant (1230–96), known as the 'father of Dutch poetry', who lived in Damme from around 1270, writing his most important works there.

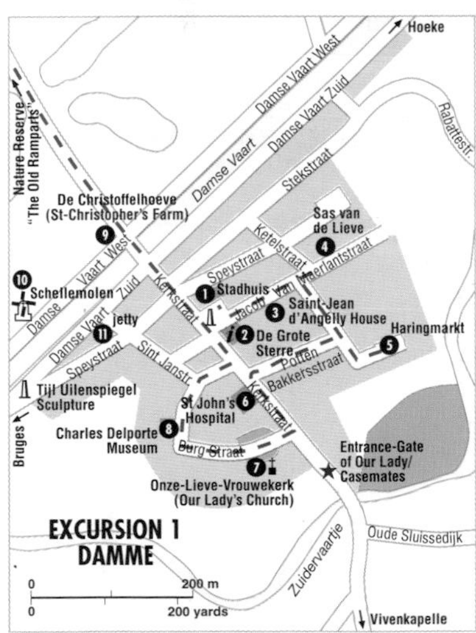

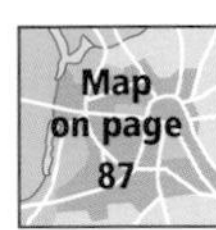

Adjacent to the Town Hall, the **Pallieter** at No. 12 Kerkstraat is a relaxed place for a drink and a snack, either inside in the atmospheric Old Flemish dining room, or outside on the terrace where you can watch the comings and goings in the Markt, when the weather is good .

Classy dining
Across the road from the Tijl Uilenspiegel Museum, De Lieve restaurant at No. 10, with a pavement terrace providing a perfect ambience in summer, is the classiest address in town for lunch or dinner *(see page 107)*.

FOLKLORE HERO

Across from the Town Hall, at No. 3 Jacob van Maerlantstraat, stands a 15th-century patrician house called **De Grote Sterre** ❷, which in the 17th century was the residence of the Spanish military governor. Restored after being severely damaged by a storm in 1990, it is now occupied by the Damme Tourist Office, the **Tijl Uilenspiegel Museum** and the **Van Hinsberg Forge and Foundry Museum** (open mid-Apr–mid-Oct: Mon–Fri 9am–noon and 2–6pm, weekends 10am–noon and 2–6pm; mid-Oct–mid-Apr: Mon–Fri 9am–noon and 2–5pm, weekends 2–5pm).

Tijl Uilenspiegel sculpture adjacent to the canal

The aforementioned Tijl Uilenspiegel is a 14th-century German folk-tale character who fetched up in Damme by a circuitous route and has since been adopted by the village. To Germans – who have the first cultural claim to him – he is Till Eulenspiegel, a pranksterish folklore hero, and a supposedly historical 14th-century peasant. Tales of this simple rustic's adventures and his practical jokes aimed at tradesmen, innkeepers, aristocrats and churchmen first appeared around 1480, in a German prose version of earlier verse romances. Damme, his 'birthplace', acquired him as a freedom fighter in Charles de Coster's epic novel *The Legend of the Glorious Adventures of Till Eulenspiegel* (1867; English 1918), which achieved international renown. In this tale, the rogue hero symbolises Flanders in its struggle against Spanish occupation.

SAINT-JEAN D'ANGELLY HOUSE

Further along Jacob van Maerlantstraat, at No. 13, is the ★ **Saint-Jean d'Angélly House** ❸, a 15th-century patrician home that was at one time the headquarters of French wine traders from the Cognac region. It was in this house in 1468 that Charles the Bold married Margaret of York, sister of England's King Edward IV, apparently because the Town Hall had not been completed in time.

Star Attraction
- St John's Hospital

Herring Market

On the corner of Jacob van Maerlantstraat and Ketelstraat are the foundations of a lock-gate, the **Sas van de Lieve** ❹, which were part of the harbour installations of the canal that was dug in the 13th century to connect Damme with Ghent.

The street opposite leads southwards to the **Herring Market** (Haringmarkt) ❺, now a lawn bordered by whitewashed and red-tiled houses, but which processed a reported 28 million herring a year from Sweden during the 15th century. Beside it are some remains of Damme's medieval fortifications, and further remains can be seen at the end of Kerkstraat, which runs south from the Markt.

Below: St John's Hospital Museum sign
Bottom: Herring Market

St John's Hospital

More interesting is the ★★ **St John's Hospital** (Sint-Janshospitaal) ❻ at No. 33 Kerkstraat, which is believed to have been endowed by Margaret of Constantinople in 1249, though probably

on an earlier foundation. As its name suggests, it used to serve as a hospital for poor sick people. The main building is Gothic, but other parts of it have been constructed in later styles.

Below: inside Our Lady's Church
Bottom: Charles Delporte sculpture outside the church

OUR LADY'S CHURCH

Also in Kerkstraat is ★★ **Our Lady's Church** (Onze-Lieve-Vrouwekerk) ❼, a squat Gothic church dating from around 1340, built over an earlier chapel from 1225. It proved to be too big for the village's needs in the straitened economic circumstances from the late 16th century onwards, caused by the Zwin silting up, and in 1725 part of it was demolished, which accounts for its truncated lines today.

Taking Burgstraat, which curves around the back of St John's Hospital, you come to the ★ **Charles Delporte Museum** ❽, containing paintings and sculptures by the Belgian modern artist. Next door, in the old schoolhouse, is **De Oede Schole** antiquarian bookshop.

THE DAAMSE VAART

Return via the Markt to the Bruges-Sluis Canal, known here as the **Daamse Vaart**. The canal was dug by Spanish prisoners of war in 1811, during the Napoleonic Wars, to connect Dunkirk with the Scheldt beyond the reach of blockading British warships off the coast.

Cross over the bridge, and facing you at No. 1 Dammesteenweg is the 18th-century whitewashed **St Christopher's Farm** (De Christoffelhoeve) ❾. Note the ornamental gate and the monumental barn with mansard roof. A little farther and you reach the **Old Ramparts** of the town walls, the line of which now forms a nature reserve.

A short way to the west along the Daamse Vaart is the ★★ **Schellemolen** ❿, a windmill built in 1867 on the site of an earlier one whose recorded history dates back to 1267.

Finally, along from the **jetty** ⓫, where the *Lamme Goedzak* docks, is a modern sculpture group recalling the legend of Tijl Uilenspiegel.

Excursion to De Haan

One of the many wonderful things about Bruges is that it lies so close to the sea – Belgium's 64-km (40-mile) stretch of North Sea coastline is just a few miles away up the E40 motorway, and indeed Bruges is the gateway to the coast. For something completely different from exploring museums, churches and Gothic architecture, the windswept beaches and sand dunes of De Haan and other coastal towns are close at hand.

Star Attractions
- Our Lady's Church
- Schellemolen

THE COAST TRAM

Access to the entire littoral is made easy by a much-loved institution, the Coast Tram (Kusttram), which runs almost the full length of the seashore from the Dutch border to the French, often no more than a few yards behind the dunes, stopping at all towns and villages along the way and at many points in between. Its 2-hour journey takes in ritzy Knokke-Heist; the seaport of Zeebrugge; the yacht harbour at Blankenberge; the beach and dunes of Wenduine; the *belle-époque* glory of De Haan; once fashionable and still popular Ostend; the busy fishing harbour of Nieuwpoort; the seafood restaurants of Oostduinkerke; and the beaches of Koksijde and De Panne, where sand-yachts excel in the abundant wind.

Below: the Coast Tram
Bottom: De Haan with the Astoria Hotel

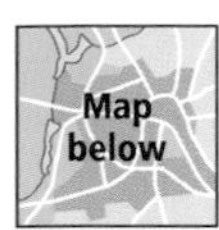

Hôtel des Brasseurs

BELLE-ÉPOQUE DE HAAN

Any one of these resorts would make a good side trip from Bruges, and each has a different character, so you are just about guaranteed to find somewhere that suits you. De Haan (called Le Coq in French) is one of the closest to Bruges, just 16km (10 miles) away, and is widely considered to be the jewel of the coast.

It is one of the few resorts that have declined to bury themselves under modern apartment blocks and hotels. Instead, many of its graceful *belle-époque* mansions have been preserved to delight the eye still, and the beach is as good as any on the Belgian coast. For many visitors this aspect more than outweighs the lack of crowds and excitement of bigger resorts such as Ostend.

THE TOURIST OFFICE

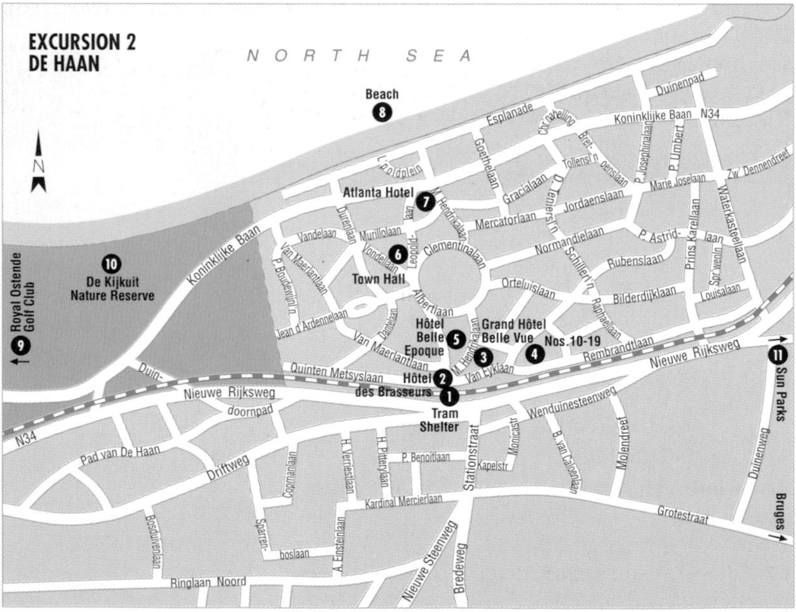

De Haan's story begins in 1888, when the Hôtel du Coq was built beside the scenic but then deserted sand dunes. As the resort began to grow up around it, strict building regulations were laid down to protect its character. The ★ **Tram Shelter** ❶ on Koninklijk Plein dates from 1902, and is interesting in itself for its Art Nouveau lines and later Art Deco decorative features. Today it houses De Haan's **tourist office**. Also in the square are two pagoda-like pavilions, now kiosks, built in 1904 for the Casino, itself erected in 1899 but since demolished.

The **Hôtel des Brasseurs** ❷ on Koninklijk Plein dates from 1900 and is another *belle-époque* gem with Art Nouveau elements. Facing it is the domed **Grand Hôtel Belle Vue** ❸, which opened in the 1920s, though it was formerly a private villa. On adjacent Rembrandtlaan, beside the tram line, is a cluster of country-style villas, **Nos. 10–19** ❹, dating from 1925–7, which have all been listed as historic monuments.

Albert Einstein
To the left of the Town Hall on Jean d'Ardennelaan, is the Savoyarde villa where Albert Einstein lived for six months in 1933. He was the guest of King Albert I and Queen Elisabeth, after he had fled from Nazi Germany.

Below: Tram Shelter
Bottom: villa in the Concession

LEOPOLDLAAN

From the Tram Shelter and Koninklijk Plein, the best way to appreciate De Haan's Art Nouveau-Art Deco heritage is to walk north along Leopoldlaan, past the **Hôtel Belle Epoque** ❺, the Art Deco **Astoria** and the extravagantly graceful **Town Hall** (Stadhuis) ❻, formerly the Grand Hôtel du Coq-sur-Mer, which was built in 1899.

Leopoldlaan leads to Koninklijke Baan, the main road running parallel to the beachfront Zeedijk-De Haan, where there are yet more buildings from the *belle-époque* period. Parallel to Leopoldlaan is Maria Hendrikalaan, where at No. 20 you can see the **Atlanta Hotel** ❼, formerly the Prince Albert Villa, built in 1901 and with later Art Deco embellishments.

THE CONCESSION

The whole central area of De Haan – known as The Concession, because it was the original zone where building was allowed – is filled with notable villas, some converted to hotels and some privately owned, all colourfully decorated. They

give a good idea of how special De Haan was when it was being developed, as indeed it still is today. As the villas are dotted all over town, it is also possible to just stroll around the centre and the side lanes leading off it rather than following any particular itinerary.

De Haan Beach

Of course, all roads lead to the ★**beach** ❽, and the mostly good open-air café terraces that line it. With safe waters and golden sands, De Haan is a popular resort for families. Part of the beach is designated for windsurfing, a popular activity here, and other sports activities include sea angling, horse riding, tennis, bowling, squash, archery, mountain biking and mini-golf.

Behind the beach on either side of De Haan are dunes and woodlands crisscrossed by signposted footpaths, and the open polderland behind that is great for cycling.

Fun park
At Sun Parks the kids can let off steam in the indoor waterpark, which is equipped with a wave machine and hydrotubes, while mums and dads soak up steam in the sauna and Turkish bath.

De Kijkuit Nature Reserve

Just west of the built-up area is the international-standard 18-hole course of the **Royal Ostend Golf Club** ❾, bordered by the dunes of the **De Kijkuit Nature Reserve** (Natuurreservaat De Kijkuit) ❿. These forested dunes are the pride of

Cricket on the beach

the local foresters (park rangers), who have managed to persuade the sand to support plant life. Should the weather be unkind – a far from uncommon occurrence on the Belgian coast – you can retreat to the 'tropics' at **Sun Parks** ⓫ in Wenduinsesteenweg, on the inland road to neighbouring Wenduine.

SEAFRONT ZEEBRUGGE

Should you find that De Haan is a mite too quiet and refined for your liking, the entire Belgian coast can be your oyster, so to speak, just by hopping aboard the Coast Tram (Kusttram). Given that you're already on a side-trip and presumably have little time available, where should you go on a side-side-trip? **Ostend** (Oostende), **Knokke-Heist** and **De Panne** are all good choices.

Ostend is closest but, being a small city, is difficult to get to grips with on a brief visit. Knokke-Heist and De Panne are at opposite ends of the Belgian coast and you'll lose considerable time getting there.

How about **Zeebrugge**? This port/resort wouldn't normally deserve to be recommended ahead of the three resorts mentioned above, but in this case there are some points in its favour. It's close, and as the port of Bruges ('Sea Bruges'), it adds to your understanding of the city that's the main focus of this book. Best of all, though, you can visit ★ **Seafront Zeebrugge**, a recently established waterfront attraction that is full of interest, especially for kids.

Foxtrot is the NATO designation for a class of diesel-powered submarine of the Soviet-era Russian fleet that are now too old and noisy for frontline work. If you have a taste for this sort of thing, you can step aboard a retired Foxtrot moored to Seafront Zeebrugge's pier, play at rushing to battle stations inside its 100-m long (330-ft) hull, and peer through the periscope.

Among other Seafront Zeebrugge attractions, you can visit the old *West-Hinder* lightship, tour an interactive exhibition on life on, below and beside the sea, and take a boat tour of the harbour.

Seafront Zeebrugge

Art

When, at the end of the 14th century, Bruges made the abrupt transition from the rule of Counts of Flanders to that of the Dukes of Burgundy, it was not long before art that reflected the new regime's cosmopolitan tastes began to appear – art so significant that it influenced the early Renaissance artists of Italy.

JAN VAN EYCK

The first major artist to make his mark in the city under Burgundian patronage was also one of the greatest painters of all time – **Jan van Eyck** (*circa* 1389–1441). Born probably at Maaseyck (Maaseik) in Limburg, Van Eyck had been employed at the court of the Count of Holland in The Hague before moving to Bruges in 1425, where he later became court painter to Duke Philip the Good.

Although he is credited with inventing oil painting, this is untrue. His use of oils was, however, revolutionary, and he brought to perfection what was still a new medium, infusing subjects with an inner glow and surrounding them with symbolic meaning. He is the first of the so-called Flemish Primitives, painters who broke away from the rigid formalism of medieval religious painting, evincing a love of nature and portraying individuals realistically.

Nowhere is this seen to better effect than in *The Arnolfini Wedding* (1434) in London's National Gallery. In a nice touch of early graffiti, the artist signed it *Johannes de Eyck fuit hic* (Jan van Eyck was here), meaning that he attended the wedding. The merchant Giovanni Arnolfini, his bride and the background of their home are presented in meticulous detail. Other key works are the *Adoration of the Mystic Lamb* (1432), a 20-panel polyptych altarpiece in St Bavo's Cathedral, Ghent, and the *Madonna of Chancellor Rolin* (1434) in the Louvre.

Fortunately, there are Van Eycks to be seen in Bruges as well. The Groeninge Museum *(see page 34)* houses the *Madonna and Child with*

Opposite: statue of Jan Van Eyck on the square that bears his name
Below: detail of Van Eyck's The Arnolfini Wedding

The Welsh connection
A strong link with Britain is evident in the Brangwyn Museum *(see page 35)*. Welsh artist William Brangwyn worked in the mid-19th century on murals in the Chapel of the Holy Blood. But it was his son Frank Brangwyn who was the success in Bruges. Born here in 1867, he returned and painted many scenes from it which, along with other items, he donated to the city.

Canon Joris van der Paele (1436), an altarpiece for St Donatian's Cathedral commissioned by the said Canon, a retired Vatican official. It shows Van der Paele being 'presented' by St George to St Donatian, while the Virgin Mary, as the Queen of Heaven, with the Christ child on her knee, looks on approvingly. Again, detail is meticulous. There is also Van Eyck's portrait of his wife, Margareta (1439), aged 33.

Petrus Christus (*circa* 1410–72), who was working in Bruges before 1440 and became a citizen in 1444, may have studied under Van Eyck. He certainly continued in the line of Van Eyck after his death, by completing some of the late master's unfinished works, and through his own paintings but with an added emotional tone. The Groeninge Museum displays his portrait of Duchess Isabella of Portugal. His *Portrait of Sir Edward Grymestone* (1446) can be seen in the National Gallery in London, and his *Nativity* (1445) at the National Gallery of Art in Washington DC.

HANS MEMLING

A giant of Flemish painters (though his cool, poetic style has left him with less of a dazzling reputation than the more popular masters), **Hans Memling** (1440–94) was born at Seliegenstadt in Germany but lived most of his life in Bruges. A

Inside the Groeninge Museum

considerable number of his works can still be seen in the city at the Memling Museum *(see page 44)*, which has among others his *Triptych of St John* (1479), the *Adoration of the Magi* (1479), and *Shrine of St Ursula* (1489). The Groeninge Museum exhibits his *Moreel Triptych.* His *Madonna Enthroned with Saints and Donors*, also known as *The Donne Altarpiece* (1468), can be seen in London's National Gallery.

After Memling, **Gerard David** (*circa* 1460–1523), from Oudewater in Holland, was the most popular artist in Bruges. He joined the Bruges Artists' Guild in 1484 and is considered to be the last of the Flemish Primitives. His dramatic masterpiece *Judgement of Cambyses* (1498) can be seen in the Groeninge Museum. Also from this period, and hanging in the Groeninge Museum, is the *Death of the Virgin* (1480) by the Ghent-based artist **Hugo van der Goes**.

PAINTERS IN BRUGES

With the development of Renaissance art, the artistic focus in Flanders switched from Bruges to Antwerp. Still, the artists **Jan Provoost** from Mons, **Adriaan Isenbrant** from Haarlem, and **Ambrosius Benson** from Lombardy all worked in Bruges. **Pieter Pourbus** (*circa* 1523–84) from Gouda in Holland, who settled in the city, was one of the leading Renaissance painters in the Low Countries, although his style harked back to the Flemish Primitives. His portraits of Jan van Eyewerve and his wife Jacquemyne Buuck (1551) hang in the Groeninge Museum. In addition, one of the great sculptures of the Renaissance can be seen in Bruges: the *Madonna and Child* (1506) by Michelangelo, which stands in the Church of Our Lady *(see pages 37–8)*.

Michelangelo's Madonna and Child in the Church of Our Lady

Similarly, in the baroque period, Bruges' artists were overshadowed by those of Antwerp. Works by **Jacob van Oost** (1601–71), **Jan Baptist van Meunickxhoven** (1620–1704), and Rococo artist **Jan Garemijn** (1712–99) can be seen in city churches and the Groeninge Museum. On the street are some notable sculptures by **Pieter**

Modern architecture
Bruges is often seen as a 'living museum', but this doesn't stop anyone incorporating modern elements into the cityscape. Indeed, on almost any lane you may walk down you will find interesting examples of modern architecture, particularly small-scale domestic schemes which cleverly combine existing proportions with the bold use of different materials such as steel and glass. The city is equally avant-garde when it comes to sculpture, the Leda and Zeus on Walplein *(see page 45)* being but one of many examples.

The Town Hall facade

Peper, including the Rococo pump (1761) in Eiermarkt *(see page 72)* and the statue of St John Nepomucene (1767) on Sint-Jan Nepomucenus-brug *(see page 33)*. The Groeninge Museum also houses works by the Flemish Expressionists, and by Magritte and Delvaux.

Architecture

Bruges' architecture can be summed up in a word: **Gothic**. Highly visible symbols tell the story of the city's medieval civic pride in the loudest and clearest Gothic terms. The Belfry soars no less than 84m (275ft) above the great Market Hall in the Markt, the city's commercial heart at the time. Next door, in the Burg, politics held sway, with the magnificent Town Hall inspiring the efforts of other Belgian cities, such as those of Brussels, Ghent, Leuven and Oudenaarde.

St John's Hospital, the churches of Our Lady, St Giles, St James and the Holy Saviour, and various monasteries and convents, show that the religious authorities were determined not to be left behind. Similarly, the builders of many private houses, mansions and guildhouses followed the same architectural style.

RENAISSANCE

The city was past its economic prime in the 16th century, when the **Renaissance** style began to infiltrate, brought in surreptitiously in the baggage of Italian traders and bankers who were established here. The oldest such facade that survives belongs to the Civic Registry in the Burg *(see page 23)* and dates from 1534–7, while the impressively proportioned facade at No. 33 Oude Burg, on the corner of Simon Stevinplein *(see page 42)*, dates from 1571. An interesting variation is the 1460s' Florentine courtyard of the Bladelin House *(see page 73)*.

Baroque made a slightly better showing. The church of St Walburga *(see pages 56–7)*, designed by a Jesuit priest and built from 1619 to 1643, is the finest example, and there are also the

Provost's House in the Burg *(see page 25)* built from 1665 to 1666, the interiors of St Anne's Church *(see page 58)* and the complex of Our Lady of the Pottery *(see page 69)*.

In the 18th and 19th centuries, such **neoclassical** buildings as the Palace of the Liberty of Bruges *(see page 21)* and the Fish Market *(see pages 31–2)* made their appearance. By the end of the 19th century, however, Gothic was back, in **neo-Gothic** guise; and the West Flanders Provincial House in the Markt *(see page 29)* is an outstanding edifice, built between 1887 and 1892.

Below: Baroque in the Church of St Walburga
Bottom: Art Nouveau detail

ART NOUVEAU AND ART DECO

There are only three examples in Bruges of the **Art Nouveau** style that made such a big impact elsewhere in turn-of-the-century Europe *(see page 39; page 50; page 72)*. **Art Deco** does rather worse, with only one really notable example: an office building in the north that is now the Dutch consulate *(see page 80)*, although De Haan *(see page 92)* has some good examples.

Literature

The Catholic priest and teacher **Guido Gezelle** (1830–99) was a one-man literary movement, who gave Flemish poetry a new lease of life with

Guido Gezelle

his volume *Kerkhofblommen* (*Graveyard Flowers,* 1858), a mixture of literary Dutch and the dialect of West Flanders. His ideas and beliefs brought him into conflict with the church and educational authorities, and he abandoned poetry in the 1870s in favour of writing essays and doing translations. Gezelle returned to his first love in *Tijdkrans* (*Time's Garland,* 1893) and *Rijmsnoer* (*String of Rhymes,* 1897), poems dealing with nature, religion and Flemish nationalism that show an original use of rhyme, metaphor and sound.

To learn more about the Bruges-inspired revolt against the French in 1302, read **Hendrik Conscience**'s novel *De Leeuw van Vlaanderen* (*The Lion of Flanders,* 1838). From a later period, **Georges Rodenbach**'s novel *Bruges-la-Morte* (*Dead Bruges,* 1892), tells of an Englishman's stay in the 'dead city' while he tries to recover from the death of his wife. In nearby Damme, the poet **Jacob van Maerlant** (1235–1300) wrote long didactic poems, and **Charles de Coster**'s *The Glorious Adventures of Tijl Uilenspiegel* (1867) gave the village its legendary hero *(see page 88)*.

Music, Theatre and Festivals

The superb Concertgebouw (Concert Building), which opened in 2002 at the south end of 't Zand square (tel: 050 476999), is the city's main venue for classical music and opera *(see page 55)*. At the neoclassical Koninklijke Stadsschouwburg (Royal Municipal Theatre), at 29 Vlamingstraat (tel: 050 443060), mainly Dutch theatre, and dance, are performed *(see page 65)*. Another performance venue is the Joseph Ryelandtzaal at Achiel Van Ackerplein *(see page 75)*. Smaller-scale events are often held in the elegant surroundings of the Prinsenhof *(see page 50)*.

Some of the **Festival of Flanders**, a season of cultural events throughout Flanders (last week in July and first week in August in Bruges), also takes place in these and at other venues; for example recitals are often held at the Holy Saviour Cathedral, St James's Church and other churches, and at the Stedelijk Conservatorium (Municipal Conservatory), 23–25 Sint-Jakobstraat.

Canal Festival

The triennial celebration of Bruges' canals, or *Reiefeest,* was introduced in 1959. It takes place in the evening and is a combination of historical tableaux, dancing, open-air concerts, and lots of eating and drinking, that runs over six non-consecutive days in August.

During this period the canals are elaborately illuminated – even more than usual, as no expense is spared. The next Reie Festival is in 2004.

PROCESSION OF THE HOLY BLOOD

One of the most popular and colourful events in Bruges is the Procession of the Holy Blood, a ceremony dating back to at least 1291, which unfolds every year on Ascension Day (40 days after Easter). The Bishop of Bruges leads the Relic of the Holy Blood through the streets from the Chapel of the Holy Blood in the Burg. Residents wearing flamboyant Burgundian-era and biblical costumes follow him, acting out biblical and historical scenes. These recall the story of the relic's appearance in Bruges, after it was supposedly brought back from the Holy Land by the Count of Flanders in 1150 (the larger probability is that it was brought from Constantinople in around 1205, *see page 25*). Passages from the Old and New Testaments and the Passion of Christ are also read out.

Below: Procession of the Holy Blood
Bottom: Golden Tree Pageant

GOLDEN TREE PAGEANT

The Praalstoet van de Gouden Boom (Golden Tree Pageant) recalls the sumptuous marriage in Damme *(see page 88)* of the Duke of Burgundy, Charles the Bold, to Margaret of York in 1468. A great procession and tournament was held in the Markt, and it is this that the Pageant celebrates. It is held every five years in August: the next one is due in 2007.

FOOD AND DRINK

In a country which has more Michelin star restaurants per head than France, it is no surprise that Belgian cuisine is a delight to the tastebuds. With its cooking firmly based on the country's regional traditions, it's hard to eat badly here. There are plenty of eateries and bars in busy, increasingly cosmopolitan Bruges. Restaurants here range from fast-food outlets to some seriously gourmand establishments, with a big mid-range of tasteful places. About the only generalisation you can make is that the farther you get from the centre and the less dependent on tourists an establishment is, the more likely it is that you'll find genuine Flemish taste and style. This is far from being a hard and fast rule, if only because virtually all restaurants in Bruges are dependent on tourists. Many restaurants have a *dagschotel* (dish of the day) or a *dagmenu* (menu of the day).

COMBINED CUISINES

Belgian cuisine is at times light and delicate, and at other times flavoursome and rich. Cuisine from the French-speaking Walloon region in the south of the country tends to be more substantial, more spicy and has more calories than Flemish or modern French cuisine. But today the various provincial cuisines seem less distinct than they used to be. The country's chefs have borrowed and combined elements from all of Belgium's regions.

Firmly Flemish yet still popular with the southern Walloons, Bruges' restaurants are treasuries of the full range of Belgian cuisine, from traditional Flemish dishes such as *waterzooï op Gentse wijze* (a fish stew from Ghent – although chicken is more often used nowadays than fish) and *paling in 't groen* (eel in a green herb sauce), to Walloon specialities such as *jambon d'Ardennes* (smoked Ardennes ham) and Ardennes game in season.

MUSSEL MEN

Belgians are fanatics for mussels (*mosselen* in Dutch, *moules* in French), despite the fact that they come from Holland. These Zeeland mussels are state-of-the-art, and a great steaming pot served with a side dish of *frieten* (french fries) in mayonnaise sauce is to die for. In fact, *frieten* with mayonnaise on their own bought from a stall or snack-bar make a good enough meal, or at least a filling snack, and not only for the cash-strapped; so too do waffles from a roadside stall. And if you are lucky enough to find them, don't hesitate to try a portion of hot snails from a street vendor.

The nearby coast delivers other seafood, such as herring, which are lightly salted on the boats, and eaten raw as *maatjes*. These are also delicious smoked, steamed, marinated (Nieuwpoort), in red wine (*bonne femme*), and more.

Sole makes its appearance as *sole à l'Ostendaise*. North Sea shrimps taste great, and at Oostduinkerke fishermen still catch them from the backs of sturdy 'sea-going' horses. Lobster and oysters round out the seafood platter. Oysters are usually swallowed raw and whole, but you can also eat them cooked *au gratin*. And don't forget,

Michelin stars
De Karmeliet in Bruges has remained one of a trio of Belgian restaurants with a maximum three Michelin stars (the others are in Brussels).

Belgium has a reputation for several types of vegetables, such as asparagus, chicory (Belgian endive) and, of course, Brussels sprouts.

Restaurant selection

€€€ = Expensive (over €100 for two);
€€ = Moderate (€50–100 for two);
€ = Inexpensive (under €50 for two).

De Karmeliet, 19 Langestraat, tel: 050 338259. One of three Belgian restaurants that sport a coveted three Michelin stars, this smallish place in a patrician house is a temple of fine food and excellent service, and not nearly as stuffy as it might be. **€€€.**

't Bourgoensche Cruyce, 41–43 Wollestraat, tel: 050 337926. One of the best, most atmospheric dining experiences in Bruges, in a beautiful old hotel overlooking the canal, serving Flemish regional specialities. **€€–€€€.**

De Snippe, 53 Nieuwe Gentweg, tel: 050 337070. Flemish and French specialities served in a transformed 18th-century mansion. The menu is strong on seafood. **€€€.**

Duc de Bourgogne, 12 Huidenvettersplein, tel: 050 332038. Another classic dining experience, with French-style dishes in beautiful surroundings and a canal view. **€€–€€€.**

Koto, in the Hotel De' Medici, Potterierei 15, tel: 050 443131. Japanese food in stylish surroundings. Meat is tender and savoury, vegetables have just the right degree of crunchiness, sushi and sashimi seafood is fresh and bright, and the sake is warm. **€€€.**

't Pandreitje, 6 Pandreitje, tel: 050 331190. Elegant and refined Franco-Belgian cuisine. The seafood is excellent. **€€€.**

De Stove, 4 Kleine Sint-Amandstraat, tel: 050 337835. A lot less formal but right up there in the taste stakes, with seafood and typical Flemish dishes. **€€–€€€.**

Hof ter Doest, 4 Ter Doeststraat, Lissewege, tel: 050 544082. In a sprawling farm that rose from the ruins of the former Ter Doest Cistercian Abbey, this fine restaurant combines the hallowed qualities and fresh produce of its predecessors, in an elegant country setting. **€€–€€€.**

Breydel-De Coninck, 24 Breidelstraat, tel: 050 339746. Almost sinfully tasty mussels served in several ways in a traditional Bruges setting. **€€.**

De Visscherie, 8 Vismarkt, tel: 050 330212. The speciality at this bright, professional restaurant in the Fish

Kasteel Minnewater elegance

Market square is seafood, and no one does it better. **€€€.**

Kasteel Minnewater, 4 Minnewater, tel: 050 334254. Quality menu in a château beside the Lake of Love. If the prices are less than might be expected in such surroundings, the quality is not. In fine weather you can dine outside on the waterside terrace. **€€.**

't Mozarthuys, 1 Huidenvettersplein, tel: 050 334530. You can hum along to the music of Wolfgang Amadeus while you wolf down the speciality grilled meat dishes here. The outdoor terrace on this pretty little square is a big draw in good weather. **€€.**

Bhavani, 5 Simon Stevinplein, tel: 050 339025. Quality and authentic Indian cuisine. Specialties are Madras and tandoori dishes; you also have vegetarian choices. **€–€€.**

Bistro de Schaar, 2 Hooistraat, tel: 050 335979. This rustic bistro, with a pavement terrace beside the Coupure yacht harbour, provides an entirely different experience to city-centre restaurants that are generally full of tourists. A popular and friendly neighbourhood eatery, with an open grill-fire, it serves fish and meat dishes. **€–€€.**

Lotus, 5 Wapenmakersstraat, tel: 050 331078. The hallowed atmosphere at this vegetarian restaurant just north of the Burg may be somewhat at odds with the diners' evident need to grab a quick bite at lunchtime, but this a haven of fine food and a good choice for lunch. **€–€€.**

Maximiliaan van Oostenrijk, Wijngaardplein 17, tel: 050 334723. Despite having as touristy a location as you can find in Bruges, Maximilian's achieves the creditable feat of not being entirely overpowered. Serves a good selection of tasty Flemish specialities. **€–€€.**

Pietje Pek, 13 Sint-Jakobsstraat, tel: 050 347874. Behind its Art Nouveau facade, this traditional restaurant serves up satisfying portions of its speciality cheese and meat fondues, and an eat-all-you-want menu. **€–€€.**

Brasserie Erasmus, 35 Wollestraat, tel: 050 335781. Budget food, much of it prepared with beer-based sauces (from a list of 100). This is an invariably busy yet personable place. **€.**

De Gouden Meermin, 31 Markt. tel: 050 333776. Trade a bit in terms of service for a wonderful spot on the Markt. **€.**

Graaf van Vlaanderen, 19 't Zand. tel: 050 333150. Straightforward budget eatery. **€.**

Huidevettershuis, 10–11 Huidenvettersplein, tel: 050 339506. Canal views from a welcoming restaurant serving Flemish and seafood dishes. **€.**

MEDIEVAL BANQUET

Brugge Anno 1468, Celebrations Entertainment, Vlamingstraat 86, tel: 050 347572, www.celebrations-entertainment.be. Dip into the food of the Middle Ages at the Sacred Heart Church, now converted into a theatre, and while you are plying your way through trencherman quantities of meat, cheese and bread, washed down by ale, you can thrill to actors playing aristocrats, jesters and minstrels, 'recreating' the wedding of Duke of Burgundy, Charles the Bold, to Margaret of York in 1468. Apr–Oct: Fri–Sat 7.30–10.30pm; Nov–Mar: Sat 7.30–10.30pm. **€€€.**

Damme

Gasthof Maerlant, 21 Kerkstraat, tel: 050 352952. Serves a tasty 'market menu' that varies with the seasons. **€€.**

De Lieve, 10 Jacob van Maerlantstraat, tel: 050 356630. Specialises in seasonal cuisine. **€€.**

Preserved on canvas

Still-life paintings by Flemish artists, from Breughel to Snyders, have celebrated the region's delight in the hearty food of Flanders throughout the ages.

Pallieter, 12 Kerkstraat, tel 050 354675. Half-timbered room where the speciality is saddle of lamb Dijonnaise. **€€.**

De Haan

Auberge des Rois, 1 Zeedijk, tel: 059 233018. Hotel-restaurant, right beside the beach, with a refined, French-style restaurant, and a less formal café. **€€€** and **€–€€.**
Tiffany's, 12 Zeedijk, tel: 059 236367. With sea views as good as the Auberge des Rois, but simpler menu and prices. **€.**

Belgian Beer

More than 400 kinds of beer are made in Belgium, and each has its own distinct glass. Two Bruges breweries contribute to this massive choice: De Halve Maan and De Gouden Boom. The former produces the strong and popular Straffe Hendrik; the latter the equally popular 'white' Brugs Blond, the strong Steenbrugge and Brugse Tripel. Among many other Belgian beers worth looking out for to sample are the potent Duvel (Devil) with its sensuous glass; Antwerp's De Koninck, known as a *bolleke* (little ball); and Trappist beers made by monks: Orval, Westmalle, Rochefort, Westvleteren, Sint-Benedictus and Chimay.

Nightlife

Bruges is not noted for its nightclubs. Visitors who have worn their feet to the bone during the day, touring its many sights, can mostly only hobble as far as the nearest restaurant when it comes to stepping out after dark. The city is not one of Belgium's nightlife citadels, but a small provincial town that has struck tourist gold thanks to its history and beauty. However, a few large and noisy bars are opening up for those with the wherewithal to keep going.

The big-name orchestras, opera and ballet companies are based in Brussels, Antwerp, Ghent and Liège, and though they occasionally visit, that's not quite the same thing. However, the opening of the Concertgebouw *(see page 55)* in 2002 has made a big improvement, by giving the city a world-class venue for classical music and opera.

Jenever

Belgium's 70 distilleries produce around 270 brands of *jenever,* which attract enthusiasts as knowledgeable as those of Scotland's malt whiskies. Called a *witteke*, this stiff grain-spirit is served in small, brimful glasses. Look out for Filliers Oude Graanjenever, De Poldenaar Oude Antwerpsche, Van Damme and Sint-Pol.

Cafés

't Brugs Beertje, 5 Kemelstraat, tel: 050 339616. A popular traditional café with more than 300 beers on its menu.
Celtic Ireland, 8 Burg, tel: 050 344502. popular Irish pub/restaurant with a fine position in a corner of the historic Burg; foundations of the city's 9th-century castle run through the cellars. Live music performances include Irish fiddle evenings, jazz, blues and light rock.
't Dreupelhuisje, 9 Kemelstraat, tel: 050 342421. A *jenever* specialist that stocks dozens of carefully crafted (and deadly) examples of the art.
Gran Kaffee De Passage, 26 Dweersstraat, tel: 050 340232. Elegant café fits well with Bruges' antique style.
Vino Vino, 15 Grauwwerkersstraat, tel: 050 345115. Spanish tapas served to the sound of blues music.
De Versteende Nacht, 11 Langestraat, tel: 050 343293. Read Dutch cartoon books, with a drink and some jazz.
Ma Rica Rokk, 't Zand 7–8, tel: 050 338358. This techno café is noisy enough to appeal to youthful spirits.

SHOPPING

WHAT TO BUY

Lace was once the principal product made in Bruges and is certainly the premier souvenir today. While most lace on sale is machine-made, usually in the Far East, genuine handmade lace can still be found, and some shops deal only in the handmade product (while most sell a mix of the two). Handmade lace is expensive.

Other notable Belgian products to look for, though most of them are not specific to Bruges, include modern tapestries, diamonds, ceramics, crystal (especially the hand-blown products of the Val-Saint-Lambert workshop in Liège), jewellery from respected modern designers based mostly in Antwerp and Brussels, and, if you can find them, pewter from Huy and hand-beaten copper or bronze, *Dinanderie,* from Dinant in the Meuse Valley.

For food and drink products to take home, or back to your hotel, there is Bruges' own **Oud-Brugge** cheese, as well as others of Belgium's 300 or so different artisanal cheeses; any of more than 400 Belgian beers, making sure to include some from the local De Halve Maan and De Gouden Boom breweries *(see pages 45 and 64)*; a bottle or two (preferably a stone bottle) of the 270 or so brands of *jenever* made and sold in Belgium; and an inexhaustible variety of handmade chocolate pralines.

WHERE TO BUY

Expensive up-market shops, boutiques and department stores mostly occupy the streets lying south and west of the Markt, an area roughly delimited by 't Zand, Geldmuntstraat-Noordzandstraat and Steenstraat-Zuidzandstraat, and the main streets within it. Vlamingstraat, to the north of the Markt, also has some good shops.

Souvenir, lace and small speciality shops are to be found all over the centre. If the weather is bad you might want to confine yourself to the shopping galleries, such as the **Zilverpand** in Zuidzandstraat, **Ter Steeghere** between Wollestraat and the Burg, and **De Gouden Boom** in Wollestraat.

SHOPPING HIGHLIGHTS

Antiek Fimmers-Van der Cruysse, 18 Sint-Salvatorskerkhof, tel: 050 342025. Silverware.

Argus, 18 Walplein, tel: 050 344432. Decorative ceramic wall tiles, many with images of Bruges.

Artlux, 1 Simon Stevinplein, tel: 050 336095. Fine leather goods such as handbags and gloves.

Brugse Boekhandel, 2 Dijver, tel: 050 332952. Central bookshop selling English publications including books, newspapers and maps.

Brugs Diamanthuis, 5 Cordoeaniersstraat, tel: 050 344160. A beautiful building dating from 1518, which sells a sparkling array of fine diamonds. There's a second branch at 43 Katelijnestraat, tel: 050 336433.

Shop till you drop...

Most shops are open Mon–Sat from 9am to 6pm. Friday evening is *koopavond* (late-night shopping), when most shops stay open until 8 or 9pm. In summer many open on Sunday too. If you are looking for a bargain, the magic words to look for on shop windows are *Solden* (Sales) and *Totale Uitverkoop* (Everything Must Go). Visitors from non-EU countries may be able to claim back value-added tax (BTW) on purchases in some shops; look for a sticker on the window or door. It's worth asking, particularly if you buy expensive items.

Callebert, 25 Wollestraat, tel: 050 335061. Stylishly modern gifts at a stylishly modern price.
De Reyghere Boekhandel, 12 Markt, tel: 050 333403. Bookshop that sells a wide range of international newspapers and magazines.
De Witte Pelikaan, 23 Vlamingstraat, tel: 050 348284. It's Santa Claus (or *Sinterklaas*) time all year round in this specialist Christmas shop.
Dille & Kamille, 17–18 Simon Stevinplein, tel: 050 341180. An interesting range of household products, toys and gifts, including old-fashioned kitchen utensils, soaps, teas, dried flowers and fruits, herbs, spices and plants.
Inno, 11–13 Steenstraat, tel: 050 330603. The Bruges branch of Belgium's premier department store chain, in the centre, good for fashion and accessories.
Kantuweeltje, 11 Philipstockstraat, tel: 050 334225. A handmade lace and tapestry specialist since 1895.
Malesherbes, 3–5 Stoofstraat, tel: 050 336924. An excellent French delicatessen.
Pralinette, 31B Wollestraat, tel: 050 348383. Some of the greatest varieties of chocolates, made with syrup, roasted nuts and fruit fillings.
Selection, 10–12 Breidelstraat, tel: 050 331186. Sells a good range of handmade lace and is centrally located.
The Tintin Shop, 3 Steenstraat, tel: 050 334292. Everything you ever wanted to own – including a red-and-white-chequered Moon rocket – from Belgium's best-known comic strip.
Van Tilborgh, 1b Noordzandstraat, tel: 050 335904. The owner makes lip-smacking pralines.
Verheecke, 30 Steenstraat, tel: 050 332286. Sells some of the finest home-made pralines.

Markets

Antiques and Flea Market, Dijver (with an extension at the Vismarkt). Mar–Oct, Sat and Sun, noon–5pm. In addition to being a source of bargains and fine antiques, the market stalls' scenic setting beside the tree-shaded canal makes this also a treat for the eyes.
Markt, Wed 7am–1pm. General market set in a square built for the purpose many centuries ago.
't Zand and nearby **Beursplein**. Saturday 7am–1pm. General markets.
Fish Market, Vismarkt, Tues–Sat. Fascinating stalls in the purpose-built 1820s colonnaded market.

Chocolate delights

PRACTICAL INFORMATION

Getting There

BY PLANE

Brussels National Airport, 14km (8 miles) from Brussels, is the closest international airport to Bruges. The following airlines all fly to Brussels from the UK, British Airways (UK, tel: 0870 850 9850; Belgium, tel: 02 717 3217; www.britishairways.com); BMi (UK, tel: 0870 607 0555; Belgium, tel: 02 713 1284; www.flybmi.com); Virgin Express (UK, tel: 0870 730 1134; Belgium, tel: 070 353637; www.virgin-express.com); and Belgian carrier SN Brussels Airlines (UK, tel: 0870 735 2345; Belgium, tel: 07 035 1111; www.flysn.com).

Three trains an hour connect the airport with Brussels' Gare du Nord, Gare Centrale and Gare du Midi railway stations, from where trains leave for Bruges. A taxi to Gare Centrale costs about €35.

BY SEA

Zeebrugge is served once daily by car ferry from Hull by P&O Ferries (UK, tel: 08705 980333; Belgium, tel: 070 707771, www.poferries.com); and once every two days from Rosyth (Edinburgh) by Superfast Ferries (UK, tel: 0870 234 0870; Belgium, tel: 050 252252; www.superfast.com). You can also sail to Calais and Dunkirk and drive from there to Bruges. Another option is to take the ferry from Ramsgate to Ostend, which is just 10 minutes from Bruges by train. The service is operated by Transeuropa Ferries (UK, tel: 01843 595522; Belgium, tel: 059 340260; www.transeuropaferries.com)

BY TRAIN

Bruges railway station is at Stationsplein, 1.6km (1 mile) south of the city centre. For train information, tel: 02 528 2828. Frequent trains arrive at Bruges from Brussels (1 hour) and Ostend and Zeebrugge (15 minutes). Destination boards say 'Brugge'. There is also a service to and from Lille in northern France, connecting with the Eurostar trains (www.eurostar.com) from London and the TGV from Paris, from where you can also take the Thalys high-speed train (www.thalys.com) through Brussels direct to Bruges, or cheaper international and inter-city trains, changing in Brussels.

The international train from Cologne to London, via the ferry at Ostend, stops in Bruges. From Amsterdam to Bruges, you have the choice of travelling via Antwerp and Brussels, with the high-speed Thalys or regular international and inter-city trains.

BY BUS

Eurolines operate two daily return services from London's Victoria Coach Station, via the Channel Tunnel's Le Shuttle train, to Bruges bus station, which adjoins the railway station (UK, tel: 08705 808080; Belgium, tel: 02 274 1350; www.eurolines.com). Eurolines buses also serve Bruges, generally via Brussels, from Paris, Cologne, Amsterdam, and most other important European cities.

BY CAR

Bruges can be reached from Brussels and Ostend on the A10 (E40), Zeebrugge on the N17, or via the Channel Tunnel and French Channel ferry ports, on the A1 in France, and A18 and A10 (E40) in Belgium.

Getting Around

BY BUS

The main city bus stations are at Stationsplein by the railway station and 't Zand, southwest of the centre, while in the centre many buses stop at or near the Markt. Schedules are prominently displayed. A single ticket *(enkele)* purchased from the driver costs €1.50 or €1.20 from a ticket office. A 10-journey pass costs €8 and can be bought at the kiosks outside Bruges Railway Station, at 't Zand or on the bus. For further information, tel: 070 220200.

Parking

Bruges has taken steps to block the flow of private cars through the old city centre. Cars are funnelled on to one of five one-way roads leading to and from the ring road. The message in the centre is: 'Don't drive.' Illegally parked cars, or those that have outstayed their welcome at a meter, stand a good chance of being clamped or towed away.

You can leave your car at your hotel car park; at four free car parks near the railway station; or six underground car parks operated by Interparking (tel: 050 339030) on the edge of the city centre, which are reasonably priced at €8.70 per day (Biekorf-Naaldenstraat; Silverpand-Dweersstraat/Zilverstraat; Begijnhof-Katelijnestraat; Pandreitje; Centrum-'t Zand); at the Station Park & Ride for €2.50; or at a free parking zone outside the centre.

Damme and De Haan

For tourist information from the two excursion destinations in this book, contact Toerisme Damme, 3 Jacob van Maerlentstraat, 8340 Damme, tel: 050 288610; fax 050 370021 (www.vvdamme.be; e-mail: toerisme@damme.be); and Toerisme De Haan, Koninklijk Plein (Coast Tram shelter), 8420 De Haan, tel: 059 242135; fax: 059 242136 (www.dehaan.be; e-mail: toerisme@dehaan.be).

Taxis

The main taxi stands are at the Markt, tel: 050 334455, and at Stationsplein outside the rail station, tel: 050 384660.

Car Rental

Hiring a car in Bruges is not a good idea because going by car is the worst possible way to get to the city's sights. If you must, Hertz is at Pathoekeweg 25, tel: 050 377234; Avis is at Koningin Astridlaan 97/7, tel: 050 394400.

Bike Hire

Recent traffic control measures have made cyclists privileged road users, and many (but not all) of the narrow, one-way streets in the centre they can travel in both directions. Many hotels offer bikes for hire. So does the railway station, at €9.50 a day, with reduced daily rates for more than one day, from the station's Baggage Depot, tel: 050 302329. Other locations with bikes for hire, at €5–9 a day, are 't Koffieboontje, 4 Hallestraat; Eric Popelier, 14 Hallestraat; De Ketting, 23 Gentpoortstraat; and Bauhaus Bike Rental, 135 Langestraat. Go carefully, because the streets are crowded with pedestrians, many of whom are liable to step out in front of you without looking.

Facts for the Visitor

Tourist Information

Efficient and friendly, Toerisme Brugge, 't Zand 34, 8000 Brugge, tel: 050 444646; fax: 050 444645 (www.brugge.be; e-mail: toerisme@brugge.be) has a wealth of information on Bruges and environs, including maps, and some of it is free. It helps with accommodation and organises tours. Open daily 10am–6pm, Thur to 8pm. Its free monthly *Exit* magazine and annual brochure *events@brugge*, list events happening in the city. The office, located in the new Concertgebouw, also organises ticket bookings.

What's on

The free monthly newsletter, *Exit*, and annual brochure *events@brugge* are available in English from the tourist office *(see page 112)*, hotels and at performance venues. The monthly *Brugge Cultuurmagazine*, also free and available from these locations, is in Dutch but performance dates and venue details are fairly easy to understand and follow.

CURRENCY EXCHANGE

Belgium's currency has been the euro (€) since its introduction in 2002. Each euro is comprised of 100 cents. There are six euro banknotes: 5, 10, 20, 50, 100 and 500 euros; and eight euro coins: 1 cent, 2 cents, 5 cents, 10 cents, 20 cents and 50 cents, and 1 and 2 euros.

The easiest way to obtain cash is with a debit/credit card and a pin number at one of the many ATM machines in the city centre. These are called 'Bancontact' and 'Mister Cash' and they can be accessed by foreign credit/debit card holders and cards linked to the Cirrus and Plus networks, plus some also by the major charge-card holders. BBL Bank, 18 Markt, has an ATM that is convenient but often busy.

Most shops and restaurants accept credit cards. For visitors from outside the Euro Zone, practically all Belgian banks will change foreign currency and travellers' cheques, but will charge a small commission. Rates can also vary from bank to bank and it is worth shopping around.

Bruges has no American Express or Thomas Cook office. The exchange desk at Toerisme Brugge gives fair deals and is open the same hours as the tourist office.

SIGHTSEEING TOURS

The best way to see Bruges must be from the open-topped canal boats that ply the waterways daily between 1 March and mid-November from 10am to 6pm, and at weekends and on public holidays, and in holiday periods from mid-November to end December and February (ice permitting). They give an unforgettable view of the old city.

The 32-minute trips cost €5.70 for adults, €2.80 for children aged 4–11 accompanied by an adult. It can be chilly on these tour-boats, and even on warm, sunny days you may need to wear a pullover or jacket; in any other

Enjoying the sights from the canal

kind of weather, warm and/or weatherproof clothing is essential.

Another good way to see the sights is by horse-drawn carriage, leaving from the Markt (or Burg on Wednesday morning). The half-hour tour, with imformative commentary by the driver, costs €30 per carriage and €13.75 for each extra 15-minute period.

De Brugse Paardentram (tel: 050 336136) operates tours by horse-drawn tram, but only by prior reservation and not on a fixed itinerary or schedule.

A 50-minute minibus tour of the city departs every hour daily between 10am and 4–7pm, depending on the month, and costs €11.50 for adults, €6 for children. Contact Sightseeing Line, tel: 050 355024. The same company runs excursions to Damme, going there by bus and returning on the paddle steamer *Lamme Goedzaak,* at €6.70 for adults and €4.70 for children.

If you'd rather walk, the tourist office can arrange a guide costing €45 for a two-hour tour, and €22.50 for each additional hour. In July and August you can join a guided tour at 3pm from the tourist office for €6, under-12s free. Tours on tape in English are available from Toerisme Brugge for one or two people.

Toerisme Brugge produces a brochure, *5 Times Bruges by Bike,* with details of city routes. For off-road cycling tours, contact QuasiMundo Bike Tours Bruges, tel: 050 330775.

They're only words...

The people of Bruges (and the rest of Flanders) speak Dutch. Behind this simple statement lies a thicket of complication. There is no such language – the word reflects the historical English inability to distinguish between the languages (and peoples) of Germany (Deutsch) and the Low Countries (Nederlands), and their lumping of them together and corrupting it to Dutch.

To English speakers, Dutch is the language of Holland and Flemish is the language of Flanders: simple. But to the 'Dutch', Nederlands is the language of Nederland (the Netherlands), of which Holland is but a part, and they are Nederlanders, not Dutch at all. To Flemings, *Vlaams* (Flemish) is not a separate language, and certainly not a dialect, with its connotation of second-class status – but an equal variant of Nederlands.

The language academy of Flanders calls this 'Netherlandic', but is willing to live with Dutch as an internationally accepted substitute, provided no one falls for the implication that it belongs to the Netherlands alone.

We can say, then: 'The people of Bruges speak Dutch.' Most speak pretty good English, too. However, don't be tempted to practise your French even though it is one of Belgium's own languages. For while Flemings speak French when necessary, the Belgian language divide dictates that if English is your first language, most will prefer to speak English with you rather than French.

Opening Times

Main museums are open Tues–Sun 9.30am–5pm. Churches and smaller museums generally have more restricted times, including a lunch break.

Banking hours are Mon–Fri 9am–5pm (some until 7pm on Thur). Shops are generally open Mon–Sat 9am–6pm, Fri until 9pm *(see page 109).*

Post and Telephone

The main post office is at 250 Markt, tel: 050 368597 (open Mon–Fri 9am–6pm, Sat 9am–3pm). The telephone area code for Bruges is 050, which (as with all Belgian area codes) must be used, even when calling a number within Bruges.

Most phoneboxes take telecards of a variety of Euro values which can be bought at post offices, Belgacom offices and many newsagents; some boxes take coins.

To call Britain, dial 00 44 then the area code minus the initial 0, then the subscriber number. For directory enquiries in Belgium, tel: 1207 or 1307; for international, tel: 1405.

DISABLED ACCESS

Bruges is not access-friendly for disabled people, although the fact that the centre is largely pedestrianised does simplify getting around for wheelchairs. Many museums and churches can easily be entered, but transport is problematic. Ring Toerisme Brugge, tel: 050 444646 for details.

EMERGENCIES

To call the police *(politie)*, tel: 101; for non-emergencies, the main police station is at 3 Hauwerstraat, tel: 050 448844.

To call the fire department or ambulance, tel: 100. For doctors on weekend and night duty, call the tourist office or the main police station. Hospitals: Academisch Ziekenhuis Sint-Jan, 10 Riddershove, tel: 050 452111; Stedelijk Ziekenhuis Sint-Lucas, 29 Sint-Lucaslaan, Assebroek, tel: 050 369111.

MEDICAL

Visitors from the EU have the right to claim health services available to Belgian nationals. Visitors from the UK should obtain an E111 from the Department of Health before leaving home. Medical care must be paid for at the time of treatment and the cost recovered when you return home.

Bruges for Children

Lots of things on offer in this beautiful city are bound to appeal to children. What could be more fun than a canal-boat cruise, tour by horse-drawn carriage or tram and trips along the canal on a paddle steamer *(see page 87)*?

Travelling fair

A big travelling fair, with rides ranging from moderately white-knuckled to modest for tots, plus fairground stalls and other attractions, is a frequent visitor to 't Zand and surrounding streets in the summer *(see page 54)*; check with Toerisme Brugge for details, tel: 050 448686.

Children might also enjoy the marvellous view of the city from the 84m-(275ft-) high Belfry *(see page 27)*, although there are 366 steps and the stairway is narrow, steep and often crowded. The tower's 47-bell carillon is fascinating to see in action. The Municipal Folklore Museum *(see page 61)* also has lots of interest, including a chance in summer to play some antique folk games of Bruges and Flanders. Not far away is a cluster of windmills *(see pages 79–80)*.

If you're in town on Ascension Day, the kids might like to see the Middle Ages and biblical times brought to life in the Procession of the Holy Blood *(see page 103)*. They can watch lace being made by hand at the Lace Centre *(see page 60)*, while the 'Brugge Anno 1468' medieval dinner *(see pages 71 and 107)* helps bring the city's history to life, though it may finish too late for young children.

Alternatively, there is a vast range of amusements and a dolphin show at the Boudewijn Theme Park *(see page 82)*. Or quieter thrills can be enjoyed at the Zeven Torentjes (Seven Towers) Farm *(see page 85)*.

In summer, the excursion to the seaside resort of De Haan *(see pages 91–5)* is bound to be a firm favourite, as the beach here is excellent and the sea is safe for bathing; plus there are some of the popular seaside things to do, like playing mini-golf and hiring pedal-powered buggies.

ACCOMMODATION

Unlike in modern cities, which have hotels that are by and large more concerned with their own sense of style, in Bruges your hotel is most likely to be a genuine complement to the city's sense of its history and worth.

There are few de luxe but soulless, business-only establishments and equally few sleazy joints at the bottom end. Whatever their star-rating, all the lodgings listed below have something that sets them apart from even the generally excellent run of their peers.

You'll find a good range from luxury to budget, and as long as you book in advance and it's not a peak period, you'll probably get what you want. If you arrive with no place to stay, the tourist office can help *(see page 112)*.

Hotel selection

In the recommendations below, price approximations are for a double room per night are as follows:
€€€€ = over €200,
€€€ = €140–200,
€€ = €70–140,
€ = under €70.

City
€€€€

Crowne Plaza Brugge, 10 Burg, tel: 050 446844; fax: 050 446868 (www.crowneplaza.com/bruggebel; e-mail: hotel@crowne-plaza-brugge. com). Has excellent guest rooms and reliable amenities, which include an indoor swimming pool, and is conveniently located right in the historic Burg square. You can visit remains of the 10th-century Romanesque St Donatian's church in the hotel cellars.

De Snippe, 53 Nieuwe Gentweg, tel: 050 337070, fax: 050 337662, www.desnippe.be (e-mail: info@desnippe.be). Not far from the Begijnhof, this 18th-century hotel has atmospheric rooms and one of the best restaurants in Bruges.

Sofitel Brugge, 2 Boeveriestraat, tel: 050 449711, fax: 050 449799 (www.sofitel.com; e-mail: h1278@accor-hotels.com). Big rooms and an atmospheric setting in a 300-year-old monastery just off bustling 't Zand square add to the character of this chain hotel.

Die Swaene, 1 Steenhouwersdijk, tel: 050 342798, fax: 050 336674 (www.dieswaene-hotel.com; e-mail: info@dieswaene-hotel.com). Built around an 18th-century

Hotel in Damme

guildhouse, and with a great canalside position facing the Palace of the Liberty of Bruges, this is a special place to stay.

€€€

De' Medici, 15 Potterierei, tel: 050 339833; fax: 050 330764 (www.goldentulipdemedici.be; e-mail: info@hoteldemedici.com). Part of the Dutch Golden Tulip chain, this is as much a modern business hotel as a tourist one, with the excellent Koto Japanese restaurant *(see page 106)* and an indoor swimming pool. Guest rooms are spacious and well-equipped.

Duc de Bourgogne, 12 Huidenvettersplein, tel: 050 332038, fax: 050 344037 (www.ducdebourgogne.be; e-mail: duc@ssi.be). Characterful hotel in a 17th-century canalside building in a picturesque position, near both the Markt and the Burg. Good restaurant.

Montanus, 78 Nieuwe Gentweg, tel: 050 331176, fax: 050 340938 (www.montanus.be; e-mail: info@montanus.be). Under new ownership, this former budget hotel has gone upmarket, with well-equipped rooms and a garden.

Navarra, 41 Sint-Jakobsstraat, tel: 050 340561, fax: 050 336790 (www.hotelnavarra.com; e-mail: reservations@hotelnavarra.com). A prince's residence in the 17th century, this recently modernised hotel has excellent service, and amenities that include an indoor swimming pool and a sauna.

Relais Oud Huis Amsterdam, 3 Spiegelrei, tel: 050 341810, fax: 050 338891 (www.oha.be; e-mail: info@oha.be). A restored 15th-century canal-front building with lavishly furnished rooms and a sense of old-fashioned, but never out-of-fashion, quality.

Romantik Pandhotel, 16 Pandreitje, tel: 050 340666, fax: 050 340556 (www.pandhotel.com; e-mail: info@pandhotel.com). An outstanding example of Old Bruges style, with quality antique furnishings; a characterful hotel in an 18th-century mansion.

Rosenburg, 30 Coupure, tel: 050 340 194, fax: 050 343539 (www.rosenburg.be; e-mail: info@rosenburg.be). Modern and stylish, with a tranquil canal-front setting and a good vegetarian restaurant.

€€

't Bourgoensche Cruyce, 41–43 Wollestraat, tel: 050 337926, fax: 050 341968 (www.relaisbourgondischcruyce.be; e-mail: info@relaisbourgondischcruyce.be). One of Bruges' gems, with eight rooms furnished in antique style in a perfect setting in the centre. Fine restaurant.

Bryghia, 4 Oosterlingenplein, tel: 050 338059; fax: 050 341430 (www.bryghiahotel.be; e-mail: info@bryghiahotel.be). Set in the 15th-century former Easterners' House (Oosterlingenhuis) and restored in 1965, the Bryghia is an attractive mid-range, family-run hotel with an old world atmosphere.

Egmond, 15 Minnewater, tel: 050 341445, fax: 050 342940 (www.egmond.be; e-mail: info@egmond.be). Although the Egmond has only eight rooms, there is loads of ambiance in this villa with its own gardens beside the Lake of Love.

Erasmus, 35 Wollestraat, tel: 050 335781, fax: 050 334727 (www.hotelerasmus.com; e-mail: info@hotelerasmus.com). Nine nicely furnished rooms in an informal setting near the centre.

Mid-week breaks

A group of top-flight and mid-range Bruges hotels have signed up to offer 2- and 3-night mid-week packages – respectively, Royal and Value-For-Money – year round (with some restrictions). What's on offer varies according to the package but includes a room with private amenities, pre-booked meals at various city restaurants, a guided city walk, and a free guidebook. Contact Toerisme Brugge *(see page 112)* for more information.

Heritage, 11 Niklaas Desparstraat, tel: 050 444444, fax: 050 444440 (www.hotel-heritage.be; e-mail: info@hotel-heritage.com). Modern hotel in an old townhouse that still has its decorated ceiling with chandelier in the breakfast room. The rooms are small but have good facilities.

Ter Duinen, 52 Langerei, tel: 050 330437, fax: 050 344216 (www.terduinenhotel.be; e-mail: info@terduinenhotel.be). A good compromise between facilities and cost, modernity and looks in this waterfront hotel.

€

Bauhaus International Youth Hostel, 133 Langestraat, tel: 050 341093, fax: 050 334180 (www.bauhaus.be; e-mail: info@bauhaus.be). Good, youth-oriented budget accommodation close to the eastern ring canal park.

Central, 30 Markt, tel: 050 331805, fax: 050 346878 (www.hotelcentral.be; e-mail: central@hotelcentral.be). Eight plain rooms set in the heart of the city.

Fevery, 3 Collaert Mansionstraat, tel: 050 331269, fax: 050 331791 (www.hotelfevery.be; e-mail: paul@hotelfevery.be). Good central position, good value for money.

Graaf van Vlaanderen, 19 't Zand, tel: 050 333150, fax: 050 345979 (www.graafvanvlaanderen.be; e-mail: info@graafvanvlaanderen.be). A good budget choice, with a lively atmosphere and plenty of nightlife possibilities on its doorstep.

't Keizershof, 126 Oostmeers, tel: 050 338728 (www.hotelkeizershof.be; e-mail: hotel.keizershof@belgacom.net). Owned by an enthusiastic young couple who make budget travellers welcome.

Leopold, 26 't Zand, tel: 050 335129, fax: 050 348654 (www.hotelleopold.com; e-mail: info@hotelleopold.com). It offers slightly more than budget-level accommodation in a good location on 't Zand Square.

De Markies, 5 't Zand, tel: 050 348334, fax: 050 348787 (www.brugge.internetgids.be/demarkies). On the big square near the railway station, this hotel delivers good value for money.

Passage, 28 Dweersstraat, tel: 050 340 232, fax: 050 340140 (www.brugeshostels.com). Youth-orientated accommodation.

Damme

€

De Speye, 5–6 Daamse Vaart Zuid, tel: 050 548542, fax: 050 372809 (www.hoteldespeye.be). Small country hotel in an old building with modern rooms, beside the canal to Bruges.

De Haan

€€€

Auberge des Rois, 1 Zeedijk, tel: 059 233018, fax: 059 236078 (www.beachhotel.be). Fine modern hotel on the beach, built in a style in keeping with De Haan's *belle-époque* villas.

€€

Belle Epoque, 5 Leopoldlaan, tel: 059 233465, fax: 059 233814 (www.dmnet.be/epoque; e-mail: hotel.belle-epoque@skynet.be). One of the best of De Haan's old villas, now converted into a notable hotel with modern facilities, and the plus that it is close to the beach.

Grand Hôtel Belle Vue, 5 Koninklijk Plein, tel: 059 233439, fax: 059 237522 (www.hotelbellevue.be; e-mail: info@hotelbellevue.be). Another of the old villas, a superb and rather fanciful-looking domed hotel right beside the shelter for the Coast Tram.

€

De Kruishoeve, 5 Duiveketestraat, tel: 059 237355, fax: 059 235495 (www.kruishoeve.be; e-mail: kruishoeve@tijd.com). A farm hotel with modern accommodation, this is an ideal choice for families with children. Horse-riding available.

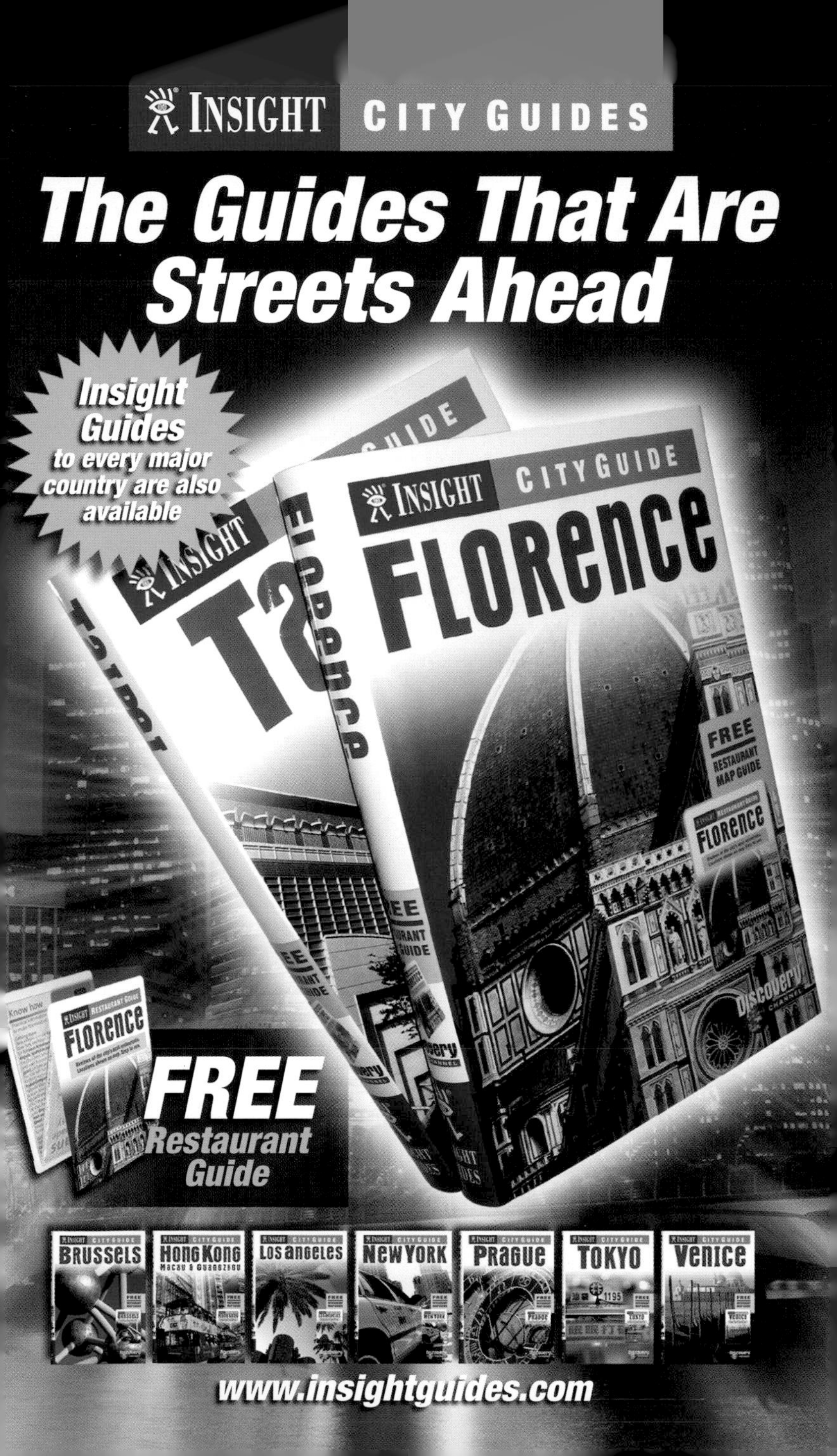

INSIGHT CITY GUIDES
The Guides That Are Streets Ahead
Insight Guides to every major country are also available
INSIGHT CITY GUIDE
FLORENCE
FREE RESTAURANT MAP GUIDE
FREE Restaurant Guide
BRUSSELS
HONG KONG Macau & Guangzhou
LOS ANGELES
NEW YORK
PRAGUE
TOKYO
VENICE
www.insightguides.com

INDEX

HotelClub

£10 OFF

Join the Club!

Earn Rewards, Get Discounts, Stay Free,
Only with HotelClub!
Across 20,000 Hotels in 97 Countries

INSIGHT GUIDES

Casa Fuster Hotel Barcelona

Pavilion Boutique Resort Samui

Register with HotelClub.com and get £10!

At ***HotelClub.com***, we reward our Members with discounts and free stays in their favourite hotels. As a Member, every booking made by you through ***HotelClub.com*** will earn you Member Dollars.

When you register, we will credit your account with ***£10*** which you can use for your next booking! The equivalent of ***£10*** will be credited in US$ to your Member account (as ***HotelClub Member Dollars***). All you need to do is log on to ***www.HotelClub.com/compactguides***. Complete your details, including the Membership Number and Password located on the back of the ***HotelClub.com*** card.

Over 2.2 million Members already use Member Dollars to pay for all or part of their hotel bookings. Join now and start spending Member Dollars whenever and wherever you want - you are not restricted to specific hotels or dates!

With great savings of up to 60% on over 20,000 hotels across 97 countries, you are sure to find the perfect location for business or pleasure.
Happy travels from ***HotelClub.com!***

www.insightguides.com